$10⁻

(49048)

Titles in this series

EDITED AND INTRODUCED BY MARY-ALICE WATERS

OUR HISTORY IS STILL BEING WRITTEN

Our History
is still being written

THE STORY OF THREE CHINESE-CUBAN GENERALS IN THE CUBAN REVOLUTION

Armando Choy
Gustavo Chui
Moisés Sío Wong

Pathfinder

New York   London   Montreal   Sydney

Edited by Mary-Alice Waters

ISBN-10: 0-87348-978-0
ISBN-13: 978-0-87348-978-2
Library of Congress Control Number: 2005909294
Manufactured in the United States

First edition, 2005

COVER DESIGN: Eva Braiman
COVER PHOTO: Members of Chinese New Democracy Alliance at
    Havana rally, September 2, 1960. Organized in response to
    Washington's efforts to line up Latin American governments
    against Cuba, the rally of more than one million approved
    a reply to the U.S. rulers known as the First Declaration of
    Havana. Banner says: "Resident Chinese support the Cuban
    Revolution and its leader Fidel Castro!"

Pathfinder
www.pathfinderpress.com
E-mail: pathfinder@pathfinderpress.com

Contents

Appendix

CUITO CUANAVALE:
A VICTORY FOR THE WHOLE OF AFRICA

Introduction

OUR HISTORY IS STILL BEING WRITTEN adds one more chapter to the chronicle of the Cuban Revolution as told by those who were—and more than fifty years later remain—on the front lines of that epic battle.

Armando Choy, Gustavo Chui, and Moisés Sío Wong, three young rebels of Chinese-Cuban ancestry, became combatants in the clandestine struggle and 1956–58 revolutionary war that brought down the U.S.-backed dictatorship of Fulgencio Batista and opened the door to the socialist revolution in the Americas. Each, in the course of a lifetime of revolutionary action, became a general in the Revolutionary Armed Forces of Cuba. Through their stories the economic, social, and political forces that gave birth to the Cuban nation and still shape our epoch unfold.

We see how millions of ordinary human beings like them—the "men and women from nowhere" who the rulers cannot even see—simply refused to accept a future without dignity or hope, refused to settle for less than they dreamed of. They marched onto the stage of history and changed its course, becoming different human beings themselves in the process.

Mary-Alice Waters, president of Pathfinder Press, is the editor of *New International*, a magazine of Marxist politics and theory. She has edited more than a dozen books of interviews, writings, and speeches of leaders of the Cuban Revolution.

The suggestion for this book originally came from Harry Villegas, himself a brigadier general of Cuba's Revolutionary Armed Forces as well as a Hero of the Cuban Revolution. Villegas is today executive vice president of the National Directorate of the Association of Combatants of the Cuban Revolution. He is known throughout the world as Pombo, the nom de guerre given him in 1965 by Cuban-Argentine revolutionary leader Ernesto Che Guevara when together they fought at the side of the anti-imperialist forces in the Congo, and over the next two years in Bolivia as well.

In February 2002 Pathfinder editors had just completed work on *From the Escambray to the Congo: In the Whirlwind of the Cuban Revolution* by Víctor Dreke. The book had been well received at the Havana International Book Fair and in spirited meetings across the former province of Las Villas in central Cuba, organized in collaboration with the Association of Combatants of the Cuban Revolution. We were already far along in preparing two more titles related to the Cuban Revolution and its place in the world: *October 1962: The 'Missile' Crisis as Seen from Cuba* by Tomás Diez; and *Marianas in Combat*, the story of Cuba's highest-ranking female officer, Brigadier General Teté Puebla, and the Mariana Grajales Women's Platoon in Cuba's revolutionary war.

Planning ahead, as a competent officer does, Villegas invited us one morning to the national headquarters of the Combatants Association and introduced us to Armando Choy, Gustavo Chui, and Moisés Sío Wong. *Our History Is Still Being Written* is the product of the work that began that day.

■

The three young Chinese-Cubans, of similar age, grew up in different parts of Cuba, under different class and social conditions. With each following his own path, all three came to the same revolutionary course of action. They threw themselves into the great proletarian battle that defined their generation—the struggle to overthrow the Batista tyranny and defend Cuba's sovereignty and independence against the onslaught of the imperialist empire to the north.

The significance and historical weight of Chinese immigration to Cuba starting in the mid-nineteenth century emerges from their accounts. In proportion to population, this immigration to Cuba was greater than anywhere else in the Americas, the United States included. In fact, thousands of Chinese laborers brought to build railroads in the U.S. West later emigrated to Cuba in hopes of finding better conditions of life and work.

The lucrative trafficking in tens upon tens of thousands of Chinese peasants—their impressment, their death-ship transport to Cuba, their indentured labor on sugar plantations supplementing the dwindling supply of African slaves, and above all their resistance, struggles, and unblemished record of combat in Cuba's 1868–98 independence wars against Spain—all that is sketched here in broad outlines. It is a story largely unknown outside Cuba.

What is presented, however, is not history alone. This is one of the indispensable strands of revolutionary Cuba today—from the pre-1959 racist oppression of Chinese as well as Blacks, to the measures taken by the popular revolutionary government headed by Fidel Castro to end this discrimination and combat its legacy, to the integration of Cubans of Chinese origin into every level of social and political life today. As Sío Wong puts it so forcefully, the greatest measure taken against discrimination "was the revolution itself."

"The Chinese community here in Cuba is different from

Peru, Brazil, Argentina, or Canada," he emphasizes. "And that difference is the triumph of a socialist revolution."

■

The revolutionary overthrow of the Batista dictatorship was not the end of a story. It was the beginning. The working people of Cuba began building a new society that posed an intolerable "affront" to the prerogatives of capital. For nearly half a century they have held at bay the strongest imperialist power that will ever stalk the globe. In doing so the Cuban toilers and their government have become a beacon, and an ally, to those the world over seeking to learn how to fight to transform their lives—and how to fight to *win*.

Among the many responsibilities Choy, Chui, and Sío Wong have each shouldered over the years within the Revolutionary Armed Forces as well as in government assignments and in the leadership of the Communist Party of Cuba, participation in Cuba's internationalist missions abroad stands out.

"Because our system is socialist in character and commitment," Choy explains, revolutionaries in Cuba have always sought to act "in the interests of the majority of humanity inhabiting planet earth—not on behalf of narrow individual interests, or even simply Cuba's national interests."

Each served in Angola at various times between 1975 and 1988, as Cuba responded to the request of the Angolan government, just gaining its independence from Portugal, for aid to defeat an imperialist-backed invasion by the armed forces of South Africa's apartheid regime.

Chui helped establish Cuba's internationalist military aid missions in Nicaragua, Ethiopia, and Mozambique. Choy served as ambassador to Cape Verde from 1986 to 1992. Sío

Wong, president of the Cuba-China Friendship Association, has helped Venezuela's toilers in their efforts to establish and extend small-scale urban agriculture.

The full story of Cuba's sixteen-year internationalist mission to Angola is still to be told. Even in Cuba, no comprehensive account is yet available. But the first-hand experiences and assessments offered here by each of these three generals provide insights into that important period in the history of southern Africa not readily available outside Cuba. Their accounts are reinforced by excerpts from speeches by Cuban president Fidel Castro in December 1988, and by Nelson Mandela and Castro in Matanzas, Cuba, in July 1991, reproduced in the appendix. The significance for Africa and the world of the March 1988 victory of the Cuban-Angolan forces over the South African apartheid military in the battle of Cuito Cuanavale is powerfully presented.

■

Our History Is Still Being Written—the title comes from Chui—captures the revolutionary perspective and ongoing intensity of work of the book's three protagonists. In the final section, "The Special Period and Beyond," each of them is looking to the future.

Today Choy heads the massive, multifaceted, multiyear project he describes here to clean up Havana Bay, and to transform the infrastructure of the port of Havana through which flows some 70 percent of Cuba's imports and 90 percent of its exports, sugar and nickel excluded. It is a task irreplaceable to Cuba's economic and social development.

Sío Wong continues to hold the responsibility he assumed almost twenty years ago as president of the National Institute of State Reserves. It is an assignment decisive not only to the current military defense of the revolution, but also to the Cuban government's ability to respond—in marked contrast, on every level, to the capitalist government of the United States—to the needs of the population in times of natural disaster such as Hurricanes Dennis and Wilma, which struck the island this year.

Chui has since 1990 shouldered national responsibilities for the founding and leadership of the Association of Combatants of the Cuban Revolution. That organization today comprises more than 300,000 Cubans with decades of experience as the backbone of the revolution—from cadres of the Rebel Army and clandestine struggle against Batista's tyranny, to young doctors and teachers completing internationalist missions around the world today, to the five Heroes of the Cuban Revolution framed up on charges of conspiracy to commit espionage and murder, now serving draconian sentences in the federal prisons of the United States. It is responsible for a political education program that reaches into every school and neighborhood in the country.

As each of the three generals makes clear, the future will be decided not *for* the working people of Cuba, but *by* them.

■

Our History Is Still Being Written, published simultaneously in English and Spanish, came together over a period of almost four years. It is the product of several rounds of interviews, some collective and some individual, that took place in February 2002 and 2004, and were completed in February and August 2005. In preparing the book for publication, we have, insofar as possible, smoothed over the discrepancies of time and circumstances that were an inevitable result of this long gestation.

When we began, for example, Sío Wong, like Choy and Chui, held reserve status as an officer of the Revolutionary Armed Forces of Cuba. By the time of our final interview in mid-August 2005, he had been called back to active duty. The enormous effort that falls under the rubric of the cleanup, preservation, and development of Havana Bay advanced considerably in the course of those four years. The damage wreaked by Hurricane Michelle in 2001 was matched or superseded by a half dozen other major storms, from Ivan to Charley to Dennis.

Most important, intensifying conflicts among contending classes on an international scale these last four years have opened a new political situation worldwide. The imperialist political offensive, spearheaded by Washington, is advancing under the banner of the "global war on terrorism" and the "transformation" of the military activity of the U.S. rulers and their allies from the Middle East to the Pacific, from Africa to Europe to the North American "homeland" itself. In response to the course of the bipartisan war party and sharpening assaults by the barons of capital, the resistance of working people, at home and abroad, is being transformed as well.

In our hemisphere, the challenges faced and surmounted by the combative toilers of Venezuela have altered the political equation. In face of inevitable aggression from the empire to the north, the stakes are being substantially raised—for us, and for the fighting vanguards of the people of Cuba, Venezuela, and throughout the Americas.

■

Arrin Hawkins, Martín Koppel, Luis Madrid, and Michael Taber each participated with me in one or more of the interviews that gave us this book. Michael Taber supervised the translation into English and prepared the glossary, annotation, and index. Luis Madrid was responsible for the manuscript in Spanish.

Production of these two books—from transcription to initial translation, from composition, proofreading, and preparation of the digital files for printing, to distribution—has been the work of more than 200 volunteers around the world who make their time and skills available through the Pathfinder Printing Project.

A special note of thanks is owed to the Biblioteca Nacional "José Martí" in Havana, including its director Eliades Acosta, assistant director Teresita Morales, and senior librarian Lisia Prieto, who is responsible for the archives that encompass the library's collection of materials related to Chinese immigration in Cuba. Aid from the library's staff was indispensable in locating and reproducing a number of the graphics that bring these pages to life.

Other historical photos and graphics were located with the help of Delfín Xiqués of *Granma*, Manuel Martínez of *Bohemia*, Milton Chee of San Francisco, California, and through the individual efforts of Generals Choy, Chui, and Sío Wong.

Iraida Aguirrechu, current affairs editor at Editora Política, the publishing house of the Communist Party of Cuba, participated at each stage in all the interviews. Without her determination, diligence, concern for accuracy, and attention to detail, this book would not have seen the light of day.

Finally, and above all, our thanks go to Generals Armando Choy, Gustavo Chui, and Moisés Sío Wong for the many hours they each made available for the work necessary to bring this book to fruition.

We are confident it will be received with thanks by those to whom it is dedicated: the new generations of fighting "men and women from nowhere" now emerging around the world, for whom the example of Cuba's socialist revolution shows the way forward.

November 2005

Cuba

HAVANA
MATANZAS

VILLA
CLARA

GUANAJAY
HAVANA

SAGUA
LA GRANDE

REMED.

PINAR DEL RÍO

PINAR DEL RÍO

MATANZAS

SANTA
CLARA

BAY OF PIGS

CIENFUEGOS

CABAIGU
FOMENTO

NUEVA GERONA

PLAYA GIRÓN
JURAGUÁ

ESCAMBRAY

SANC
SPIR

CIENFUEGOS

SANCTI SPIRIT

ISLE OF YOUTH

0   50   100 miles

United States

ATLANTIC OCEAN

GULF OF MEXICO

Bahamas

Puerto
Rico

Cuba

Jamaica

Haiti

Dominican
Republic

Mexico

Belize

Honduras

CARIBBEAN SEA

Guatemala
El Salvador

Nicaragua

Costa Rica

Venezuela

PACIFIC OCEAN

Panama

Colombia

IEGO
DE
VILA

O DE ÁVILA

CAMAGÜEY

C A M A G Ü E Y

VICTORIA DE
LAS TUNAS

L A S
T U N A S

HOLGUÍN

H O L G U Í N   MAYARÍ

MOA

BAYAMO

MANZANILLO

YARA

PALMA SORIANO

G U A N T Á N A M O

G R A N M A

S I E R R A   M A E S T R A

GUANTÁNAMO

SANTIAGO DE CUBA

U.S. NAVAL BASE

S A N T I A G O   D E   C U B A

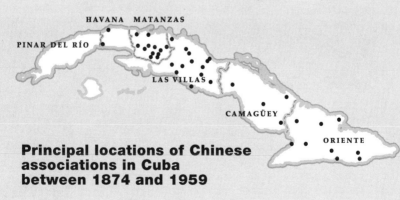

HAVANA   MATANZAS

PINAR DEL RÍO

LAS VILLAS

CAMAGÜEY

ORIENTE

**Principal locations of Chinese
associations in Cuba
between 1874 and 1959**

Based on map prepared by Fundación Fernando Ortiz

Armando Choy
during interview,
February 2004.

Above, as member of one of the revolutionary
tribunals that tried hundreds of the Batista
regime's murderers and torturers in the first
months following the revolution's triumph.
Next to Choy (at left) are Capt. Miguel Duque
Estrada and Commander Víctor Bordón.

As ambassador
to Cape Verde, 1991.

Armando Choy

BORN 1934 IN FOMENTO, Las Villas province, Armando Choy Rodríguez moved to Santa Clara with his family when he was fourteen.

Following Fulgencio Batista's 1952 military coup, Choy joined the anti-Batista organization Joven Patria (Young Homeland). He was a founding member of the July 26 Movement in 1955. At the beginning of 1958 he became provincial leader of the organization's Student Front in Las Villas province and the head of its action and sabotage activities. On April 9, 1958, he led an armed group that participated in the attempted nationwide general strike that day. As a result of his revolutionary activities he was arrested and jailed six times.

In May 1958 he joined a guerrilla unit of the July 26 Movement in the Escambray mountains led by Commander Víctor Bordón. When Rebel Army Column 8, led by Commander Ernesto Che Guevara, arrived in the Escambray in October, Bordón's unit became part of it. On December 26 of that year Guevara promoted Choy to captain, the third-highest rank in the Rebel Army.

Following the January 1, 1959, fall of the dictatorship, Choy served on the revolutionary tribunals that tried war criminals of the Batista regime. In mid-1959, when three Rebel

Army forces were created in the east, west, and center of the country, he became deputy head of the Infantry Regiment of the Central Tactical Force. In 1960 he headed the Revolutionary National Militia in Las Villas province, helping to organize the struggle against counterrevolutionary bands there.

In early 1961 Choy became payroll master of the newly formed Central Army. During the April 1961 U.S.-backed mercenary invasion at the Bay of Pigs, which was defeated seventy-two hours later at Playa Girón, Choy was head of one of the units engaged in combat, the 345th Infantry Battalion, from the current province of Sancti Spíritus.

Later that year he was assigned to organize and command the infantry division of Sancti Spíritus and later that of Trinidad, both of which participated in the campaign against counterrevolutionary bands in the Escambray mountains.

Promoted to commander in December 1962, Choy was transferred to the Anti-Aircraft Defense and Revolutionary Air Force (DAAFAR) in April 1963, and became head of the antiaircraft defense section of the Western Army. In 1973 he was named head of antiaircraft missile forces and deputy commander of DAAFAR. He was promoted to brigadier general in November 1976.

Choy participated in the internationalist mission in Angola during 1980–81. Upon his return, he served in DAAFAR's leadership until December 1986, when he was named ambassador to the Republic of Cape Verde, a responsibility he carried out until 1992.

He is currently president of the State Working Group for the Cleanup, Preservation, and Development of Havana Bay. He organizes the administration of the Port of Havana and is the representative of the minister of transportation there.

Choy retired from active duty in the Revolutionary Armed Forces in 1992. He is a founding member of the Communist Party of Cuba, and belongs to the Association of Combatants of the Cuban Revolution.

Gustavo Chui during interview, February 2002.

At left, speaking to troops in Angola, December 1987.

Chui, left, with Fidel Castro, on the occasion of Chui's promotion to brigadier general, 1980. Between them are Div. Gen. Francisco Cabrera and Brig. Gen. Línder Calzadilla.

Gustavo Chui

BORN 1938 IN SANTIAGO DE CUBA, Gustavo Chui Beltrán joined the revolutionary movement at age sixteen. He was active in the July 26 Movement's urban underground in Santiago during the first part of the revolutionary war.

In the spring of 1958 he went up to the Sierra Maestra mountains to join the Rebel Army, where he participated in a number of battles as a combatant in Column 3, commanded by Guillermo García.

Days after the revolutionary victory in January 1959, Chui was posted to Camp Managua on the outskirts of Havana, under the orders of Commander Juan Almeida Bosque. There he was assigned to an infantry battalion and then a tank company. In July 1959 he was sent to Belgium to study infantry armaments. Returning in September 1960, he was assigned as a technician in the Department of War Matériel at Camp Managua. Later he served as armaments chief of the Revolutionary Air Force.

In April 1961 he was named head of armaments in Pinar del Río province, under Commander Ernesto Che Guevara. There he was in charge of arming the militia and army units that combated counterrevolutionary bands and fought at the Bay of Pigs.

The following year he became the Western Army's head of

armaments. In 1965 he was deputy head of the Armaments Subdirectorate of the Revolutionary Armed Forces (FAR). In 1968 he became head of the FAR's Armaments Directorate.

In September 1971 he was named second in command of the 10th Directorate of the FAR, the unit responsible for Cuba's internationalist missions. In December 1975, after the death in combat in Angola of Raúl Díaz Argüelles, Chui became head of the 10th Directorate. Simultaneously he was assigned to head the staff of the Ministry of the Revolutionary Armed Forces' Special Command Post, assisting Commander in Chief Fidel Castro and Minister of the Revolutionary Armed Forces Raúl Castro in directing Cuba's internationalist mission in Angola.

Chui later was deputy head of the commission that established Cuba's military mission in Ethiopia. He also helped establish Cuban military missions in Mozambique and Nicaragua.

In 1981 he was named head of the FAR's Cadres Directorate, in charge of assigning officers and maintaining the structured chain of command.

From 1983 to 1986 he was deputy chief of the FAR's general staff.

In 1986 Chui was sent to Angola as deputy chief of staff of the military mission. In December 1987 he was named head of the 90th Tank Brigade in Malanje. In March 1988, while leading an operation of this brigade in northern Angola, he was critically wounded and lost a leg after his vehicle hit an antitank mine.

Beginning in 1990, when the Association of Combatants of the Cuban Revolution was first organized in Pinar del Río as a pilot project, and since its founding as a national organization in 1993, Chui has headed the secretariat of finances and supplies as part of the association's leadership.

He retired from active military duty in 1998.

Chui is a founding member of the Communist Party of Cuba.

Moisés Sío Wong during
interview, August 2005.

At left, as member of Rebel Army
Column 8, January 1959.

With Fidel Castro
and Carlos Lage (center),
March 1996.

Moisés Sío Wong

Born 1938 in matanzas province, Moisés Sío Wong moved with his family to Havana in 1947. He joined the fight against the Batista dictatorship as a high school student, participating in demonstrations and other protest actions. Becoming a member of the July 26 Movement soon after its founding in 1955, he led its first Youth Brigade in Havana, under the command of Gerardo Abreu (*Fontán*).

In 1957 he joined the Rebel Army in the Sierra Maestra, serving in the command post platoon of Column 1 led by Fidel Castro. He participated in the battles that defeated the Batista army's offensive in 1958. In August he was assigned to Column 8 led by Ernesto Che Guevara, and participated in the column's advance from the Sierra Maestra to Las Villas province.

Following the January 1959 revolutionary victory, Sío Wong was promoted to first lieutenant and became a founder of the Rebel Army's military police. During the invasion at the Bay of Pigs in April 1961, he was head of the 7th Infantry Division in Pinar del Río under the command of Guevara. A founder of the Western Army as first operations officer, Sío Wong subsequently worked in the Anti-Aircraft Defense and Revolutionary Air Force (DAAFAR), where his responsibilities included head of the Central Division. In 1965 he was named adjutant to Raúl Castro, minister of the Revolutionary Armed Forces, holding that responsibility for seven years.

In 1976 Sío Wong served as part of Cuba's internationalist military mission in Angola as head of logistics. In November of that year he was promoted to brigadier general. From 1982 to 1985 he headed the FAR's Cadres Directorate, in charge of assigning officers and maintaining the structured chain of command.

In 1986 he was named president of the National Institute of State Reserves (INRE), a responsibility he holds today. During 1987–88 he organized logistical support for the Cuban mission in Angola.

A founding member of the Communist Party of Cuba, Sío Wong is also president of the Cuba-China Friendship Association. As a member of the National Assembly of People's Power and its International Relations Commission, he was president of the Parliamentary Group for Friendship with China. In the early 1990s he was central to initiating the small-scale urban agriculture program that has expanded throughout Cuba. Since 2003 he has served as a consultant on a similar program initiated in Venezuela.

He retired from active military duty in 1998 and returned to active service in 2005.

PART I

'THE DIFFERENCE IS A SOCIALIST REVOLUTION'

CHINESE IN CUBA

Members of Chinese New Democracy Alliance at Havana rally, September 2, 1960. Organized in response to U.S. efforts to line up Latin American governments against Cuba, the rally approved a reply to Washington known as the First Declaration of Havana. Banner reads: "Resident Chinese support the Cuban Revolution and its leader Fidel Castro!"

Three revolutionaries

MARY-ALICE WATERS: The three of you were each part of the generation of youth in Cuba whose struggle brought down the U.S.-backed Batista dictatorship at the end of the 1950s and established the first government in the Americas that fights to advance the interests of the working classes. You yourselves were transformed by those struggles and the fight to consolidate and defend the "first free territory of the Americas."

How did you become cadres of the revolution? What was it like for each of you growing up in prerevolutionary Cuba? What discrimination did you face because of your Chinese ancestry? Why did you join the revolutionary movement?

ARMANDO CHOY

ARMANDO CHOY RODRÍGUEZ: I was born in 1934 in the town of Fomento, in what was then Las Villas province. I was one of four children, three girls and a boy.

The Fomento area was quite rich in agricultural and mineral resources, perhaps the richest in Cuba. There were two sugar mills. It was a major tobacco- and coffee-growing region, and still is. A lot of livestock too; cattle were taken to the cities for slaughter. And there were even some copper mines.

Fomento had a big Chinese community, a few of whom were quite powerful economically. A number of the large businesses were owned by Chinese. My godfather, along with another Chinese man, owned Fomento's baseball stadium, for example. He also owned a number of stores and houses. After 1959 my godfather's property interests were adversely affected by the social measures of the revolution, and he left Cuba for the United States.

My father was born in China, coming to Cuba in 1918, I believe. He was brought over by his uncle, who owned a store in Palos, in Havana province, and had a lot of money.

My father is an unusual case. He came to Cuba, went back to China, and then returned again. Among the Chinese who emigrated to Cuba, this was very rare. Clearly he would not have been able to do this if his uncle hadn't had money.

At home, when I was growing up, we spoke only Spanish. My father used to say that you didn't learn to speak Chinese unless you studied it at school.

My mother, who wasn't Chinese, was a very hard-working Cuban woman. She was a fanatical supporter of Eduardo Chibás, leader of the Orthodox Party. My father, too, admired him. Every Sunday night at 8:00 PM my father would listen to Chibás's weekly radio broadcasts, which had begun to be aired in the late 1940s.

To give you an example of where my mother's sympathies lay: When I told her I was going off to join the armed struggle in the mountains to fight the Batista dictatorship, the only thing she said to me was "Be careful." Not that I shouldn't go, but "Be careful."

In 1948, when I was fourteen years old, my parents moved to Santa Clara, the capital of Las Villas province. Back then the current provinces of Sancti Spíritus, Cienfuegos, and Villa Clara were a single province. At that time in Fomento you could study up to the sixth grade, but no further. We moved to Santa Clara so I could continue my studies.

MARTÍN KOPPEL: What did your family do?

CHOY: My father was a merchant. At first he had a grocery store. Later he became a traveling salesman, representing various importing firms. After we moved to Santa Clara, he owned a small general store.

For five years I worked in this store during the day and studied accounting at night at the Santa Clara business school. Accounting! I wasn't especially interested in it. What I wanted to study was history. But my father, who was thinking about his business, said no.

An incident when I was working at my father's store still sticks in my memory. One day around noon, a man walked in. I knew him, since he always used to pass by the store. The man came in crying. He wasn't putting on an act. He asked me to sell him a pound of corn meal on credit. It was all that he, his wife, and his two children were going to eat that day for lunch, their main meal. He asked me to advance him a pound of corn meal. I gave it to him.

"He's not going to pay you for it," my father said.

"That doesn't matter," I replied.

Do you know how much a pound of corn meal cost then? Seven cents. He didn't even have seven cents!

I recall something else from my youth that had an impact on me.

I had gone back to Fomento, perhaps on vacation, I don't recall. A friend of mine lived there, the son of a fairly well-off Chinese man and a mother who was white. He had a girlfriend whose parents were of Spanish descent.

One night there was a party in town. I remember that as we approached the Spanish neighborhood—there was a Spanish neighborhood in all the towns—he said, "Let's go to the dance."

I decided not to go along, since I never really liked dancing.

But when my friend and the girl tried to get in, they were turned away because he was Chinese. It was for whites only!

That act of discrimination convinced me of the injustice prevailing in Cuba before the triumph of the revolution.

Into the revolutionary struggle

WATERS: When did you get involved in the revolutionary struggle?

CHOY: As a student in Santa Clara. On the very day of Batista's coup d'état, March 10, 1952.

I opposed the coup and soon joined an anti-Batista organization. This was before the attack on the Moncada garrison.[1] In Santa Clara there were two revolutionary groups. One was called Acción Cívica Constitucional [Constitutional Civic Action] led by Osvaldo Herrera. And there was another group called Joven Patria [Young Homeland] led by Benigno Piñeiro, who later became a traitor. I joined Joven Patria.

I always say I'm a Fidelista going back to July 26, 1953. Because on that day, when the radio announced that Dr. Fidel Castro was the leader of the Moncada attack, I said, "That's the man we need to fight the dictatorship."

In the summer of 1955 Frank País, by then a national leader of the July 26 Movement from Santiago, came to Santa Clara to establish the organization there. I didn't meet him. But that's when the July 26 Movement was organized in the city, and the majority of us young people went over to it. The organization locally was led by Quintín Pino Machado. He was a great leader, who later became a political officer with us in

1. For the Moncada attack and other historical events and figures referred to throughout the interview, see glossary starting on p. 187.

the Revolutionary Armed Forces.

I was a student leader and helped organize action and sabotage activities. I participated in student struggles and took part in street demonstrations, strikes, and other actions. I was jailed several times.

ARRIN HAWKINS: What for?

CHOY: From the moment I joined the July 26 Movement, I became more and more action-oriented—starting with the most simple tasks, such as painting slogans on walls against the Batista dictatorship and participating in student demonstrations. At the beginning these demonstrations were relatively peaceful. But as the 1950s progressed they usually ended up in fierce physical encounters with the army's Military Intelligence Service (SIM) and with the police. I also participated in sabotage actions, using Molotov cocktails and Brazilian grenades, although we could never get those grenades to explode.

As a result of these activities, I was arrested and jailed six times. Twice I was brought to trial before the Urgency Court.[2] I was acquitted both times.

At the beginning of 1958 I was named head of the July 26 Movement's Student Front in Las Villas province. That's what I was doing up to April 9, in addition to heading two action and sabotage units.

WATERS: April 9, 1958, is the day the July 26 Movement called a nationwide general strike against the dictatorship.[3] It

2. See glossary, Urgency Courts.

3. See glossary, April 9 general strike attempt. For accounts of the April 9 events by leaders of the July 26 Movement's urban underground, see Armando Hart, *Aldabonazo: Inside the Cuban Revolutionary Underground, 1952–58* (Pathfinder, 2004). The reorganization of the July 26 Movement following the April 9 events is described in the chapter "A Decisive Meeting" in Ernesto Che Guevara, *Episodes of the Cuban Revolutionary War, 1956–58* (Pathfinder, 1996).

failed utterly. What happened in Santa Clara that day? What were you doing?

CHOY: Groups of young workers and students were waiting to receive arms that morning, so that at the agreed-upon signal—which was to be the ringing of the bell of La Pastora Church at 11:00 AM—we would head out into the streets to support the strike. In fact only one group, that of the Condado barrio, received rifles. Another group, composed of students from the business high school and commanded by me, received four pistols.

Our compañeros were supposed to ring the church bell, but they never did. The Condado group, together with ours located in the La Pastora barrio, went out into the street without receiving the signal. The Condado group fought courageously against the dictatorship's army and police, and several experienced clandestine fighters—Antonio Aúcar Jiménez, David Díaz Guadarrama, and Héctor Martínez Valladares—were killed. Later on another of these valiant combatants, Eduardo "Bayoya" García, was captured and murdered by the tyranny's henchmen.

Since we never got the signal, the only thing our group of combatants from the business high school did was disarm a lone policeman.

It was lucky our compañeros didn't ring the church bell, however. Had we gone off to try to block the movement of the army and police with just five handguns—four pistols plus the revolver taken from the cop—we'd have been killed for sure. There was too great a disparity of weapons. But I was young and didn't stop to think about things like that too much.

From that day on, I was totally underground.

At the end of April the movement transferred me to the city of Cienfuegos. While I was hiding out in Santa Clara, they told me that Aleida March—an outstanding fighter who joined the armed struggle in the mountains and later was married to Che Guevara—would come see me on such and such a day. She and I were comrades in the clandestine struggle then. So she came and told me, "OK Choy, tomorrow someone will come get you." I think the person's name was Morejón, a driver who worked near my house and was in the July 26 Movement. Two others were in Morejón's car, both from Sagua la Grande on their way to Cienfuegos. One was Víctor Dreke. The other was named Garrido, whose brother had been killed in Sagua. Garrido was no good—he was a coward and a half—and he later turned traitor. Dreke, however, was quite a good combatant and compañero, as we know.[4]

In Cienfuegos they checked us into a clinic as patients. I recall that a revolutionary nurse named Víctor gave me the name Armando Pi.

"Why are you giving me a Spaniard's name?" I asked him. "Give me a Chinese last name. Because they're going to find me out with that one."

"Look, if they figure out who you are, they'll kill you anyway," Víctor told me. "So keep the name we gave you."

From Cienfuegos I went up to the mountains.

Taking up arms

KOPPEL: What happened after you got there?

CHOY: A front of the July 26 Movement, led by Commander Víctor Bordón, had recently been opened in the Escambray mountains. I became a member of this guerrilla unit on May 9, 1958. I was the nineteenth member. I joined as a simple combatant and was promoted to lieutenant by Bordón in August.

---

4.   For Dreke's own account of this episode and much more, see *From the Escambray to the Congo: In the Whirlwind of the Cuban Revolution* (Pathfinder, 2002).

This guerrilla column is a little-known chapter of the July 26 Movement in Las Villas. We had six combat engagements before being integrated into the column led by Commander Che Guevara in October 1958. In fact, my first San Cristóbal automatic rifle was seized by us during an ambush we carried out in the Mandulo region, located in what's today the province of Cienfuegos.

We had serious frictions with another organization there called the Second National Front of the Escambray, which had betrayed the Revolutionary Directorate and split from it. The majority of its soldiers were OK. But its main officers were bandits, and later, after 1959, they also became counter-revolutionaries. That's the reality, as events showed. They wound up being part of imperialism's forces.

In October 1958 we received orders to march eastward through the mountains to join up with Che, whose column had just arrived after a difficult trek from the Sierra Maestra.[5] Our march to meet them lasted about two days. It had to be undertaken very carefully, since we thought we were going to have a confrontation with the Second Front of the Escambray. Fortunately there was no such encounter, as it would have been painful to suffer deaths from a struggle within the ranks of revolutionary combatants. I was named second in command of the forward detachment, which had sixty-five combatants under Captain Cente—Edelberto González.

When we got to an area called Las Piñas, Che spoke to us.

5. For an account of the Rebel Army columns led by Che Guevara and Camilo Cienfuegos that marched from the Sierra Maestra in eastern Cuba to Las Villas province in the center of the island during September–October 1958—in what is known in Cuba as the "invasion"—see Guevara, *Episodes of the Cuban Revolutionary War, 1956–58*, "From Batista's Final Offensive to the Battle of Santa Clara," and "The Las Villas Campaign, September–December 1958."

That's when we began joint operations.

In December Che promoted me to captain and assigned me a platoon of twenty-six new combatants. As a member of Che's column, I participated in a number of battles that contributed to the Rebel Army's liberation of Las Villas province. That offensive culminated in the battle for Santa Clara, which ended on January 1, 1959, when Batista fled.

I was then ordered to be part of the advance on Havana with Bordón's column, reinforcing Column 2, under the command of Camilo Cienfuegos. On January 2 we reached Matanzas and took the surrender of the army's regiment there. Later that day we reached Havana and accepted the surrender of Camp Columbia, the old army's main military camp. The following day I was reassigned to Che's column.

WATERS: Did the fact that you are of Chinese descent have an impact on the development of your revolutionary consciousness?

CHOY: Not really. Clearly, being the son of a Chinese parent fostered a special warmth toward China, and I greatly admire that country and its heroic and selfless people. But I joined the movement as a Cuban. I thought like a Cuban, not like someone from China.

I was coordinator for the July 26 Movement's Student Front in the old province of Las Villas. The leading Cubans from the other high schools accepted me as any other Cuban. Within the movement there was no discrimination.

GUSTAVO CHUI

WATERS: General Chui, you grew up in Santiago de Cuba, in eastern Cuba. Was your family background similar to Choy's?

GUSTAVO CHUI BELTRÁN: No, it was quite different. In Santiago there was a Chinatown composed of a fair number of Chinese and their descendants, although it was smaller than Havana's.

My father, José Chui, got together with my mother, Ana Hilda Beltrán, who was a poor black Cuban. After I was born there was a conflict between the two, primarily because my father's closest compatriots were opposed to the marriage owing to the racial prejudices of the time. This was especially true of my father's main business partner, with whom he owned a grocery store. My father and his partner went to court to change my birth certificate. I had been born in 1938, but they put down I'd been born two years earlier, in order to take away my mother's parental rights. They paid off a lawyer to do this. My mother, a poor black woman, lacked the economic means to prevent it. Because of this, I remained under my father's care. I learned all this only when I was older, after my mother had died.

At that time we lived in the grocery store, together with the other Chinese who worked there. I spent most of my time in the backyard. I never went out and had nothing to do with other children in the neighborhood. As a result I spoke Cantonese only, not Spanish. One reason for all this was to keep me away from my mother.

We lived in the neighborhood of Los Olmos in Santiago de Cuba, through which General Wood Street runs (now it's René Ramos Latour Street). Our house was across the street from the Rubio canvas shoe factory (today it's a textile mill).

When I was about five years old, they let me go out into the neighborhood for the first time, and I began playing with other children my age. But the other kids couldn't understand me, and I couldn't understand them. They'd speak to me in Spanish and I'd answer in Chinese. Everyone would laugh at me. So I found a way to learn Spanish and started forgetting Chinese. Even when my father spoke to me in Chinese, I'd answer him in Spanish.

Among the Chinese I was called Conchan. So the children called me that too. That's what most of my relatives and friends in Santiago de Cuba still call me.

My father had no more children in Cuba. Before he came over from China, he'd had a few children, but I don't know anything about them. That's not the case with my mother. She had another son, my brother Jorge Luis, who lives in Santiago de Cuba.

My father's main partner, Arsenio Hung, had a large family, and I was counted as the oldest son, since I helped care for his children for a period of time. What's more, owing to my father's changes of jobs, at times I lived with the families of other Chinese who were partners of his. During my childhood I had three foster mothers, and I ended up with a large number of foster brothers and sisters.

My father was a merchant, as were most Chinese who lived in Santiago. The most common businesses were stores, small restaurants, bakeries, laundries, bars, vegetable stands, things like that.

My father and Arsenio had a grocery store that went bankrupt. Later they bought a bakery in the Sierra Maestra, in a place called San José de Aserradero, but it too failed.

My father and I had to move to Havana, this time at the urging of my cousin Rafael Wong, who owned a candy shop on Manrique Street, where today there's a day-care center. After my cousin sold the candy shop, he bought a bar on San Rafael Street. Later he sold the bar and bought the Chan Li Po cafeteria on Virtudes Street. For two years I lived with this family, under the care of Barbarita, one of my foster mothers.

In Havana I studied at the Sara Madera school and later in the Campos school, both in the Lawton neighborhood, where my father's cousin and his family lived.

WATERS: Did you maintain any contact with your mother while you were growing up?

CHUI: I learned afterward that she used to watch me from afar, since she feared running into my Chinese family, who had threatened her and told her to keep away from me.

I was in Havana in 1945, when the Second World War ended. I remember this because of the little tune they used to sing back then: "Bim bim, there goes Berlin. Bam bam, there goes Japan." Arsenio asked my father to return to Santiago, since he had a new bakery, La Cubanita, in the Sueño neighborhood; it still exists. By then Arsenio was married and had a number of small children. This was one of the more stable situations I lived in, and I did so for some ten years.

My father and his partner sold this bakery and bought another one, called Las Américas, located in the same neighborhood, and it too is still there. I began to go to the San Lucas Episcopal School in front of Maceo Stadium, where I studied until seventh grade.

This buying and selling of bakeries turned out to be quite frequent for my father and Arsenio Hung. Because of this, we covered a lot of ground in Santiago. Among the bakeries I can point to are La Moderna, in the Sorribe neighborhood, and Nueva China, close to the Spanish neighborhood in Alto de Quinteros.

July 26 Movement cadre

HAWKINS: What attracted you to the revolutionary movement?

CHUI: My father and his Chinese partners lived relatively comfortably, and I didn't experience hard times. But I always sensed the social and political atmosphere around me in the various barrios I lived in.

Events such as the 1952 coup d'état by dictator Fulgencio Batista shook the people, especially the youth. After the attack on the Moncada garrison, we were becoming more and more conscious of the unjust character of that merciless regime.

At the beginning of 1957 I joined the July 26 Movement. I became part of a cell led by Miguel Mariano Martínez Hierrezuelo, a revolutionary fighter who later became a Rebel Army captain.

Initially I participated in action and sabotage activities. The first missions consisted of obtaining food supplies and medicines for the revolutionaries who were being hidden or were wounded. Later I distributed propaganda, placed homemade bombs, and engaged in other activities that expressed our spirit of rebellion, our willingness to fight to overthrow the tyranny. I carried out these types of missions until shortly before the strike of April 9, 1958. After that I went up to the Sierra Maestra, where I joined the "Mario Muñoz Monroy" Third Front led by Commander Juan Almeida Bosque.

I should stress that it was one of my foster mothers, Lidia Wanton, who took me there. She was married to Antonio Fong, one of my father's Chinese friends, and they had a small farm in the Sierra Maestra called El Lucero. At the insistence of her son, who was already a member of the Third Front, she came to Santiago to get me.

When I reached the Sierra, I went before Captain Enrique López in La Anita camp. I became part of the troops under the command of Lieutenant Idelgarde Rivaflecha, who was known as Jabao Cuchillo. After the Batista army's summer 1958 offensive was over,[6] I became part of the "Santiago de

6. Taking advantage of the momentum gained from the collapse of the April 9, 1958, strike, the Batista army sent 10,000 troops into the Sierra Maestra, in an attempt to annihilate the revolutionary

Cuba" Column 3, led by Commander Guillermo García.

As a member of this column I participated in a number of battles and skirmishes, among them the capture of Palma Soriano, which initiated the preparations for the planned attack on Santiago de Cuba. On January 1, 1959, as the column was heading off toward its objective—while we were in the village of Escandel—we learned that the army of the tyranny had surrendered.

Now victorious, we entered Santiago de Cuba, and on the night of January 1 my platoon was assigned to guard Céspedes Park. It was from there that the commander in chief spoke to the people of Santiago de Cuba and the entire nation.

We then left on the Liberty Caravan en route to Havana, with Fidel at the head.[7]

MOISÉS SÍO WONG

WATERS: General Sío Wong, you grew up in Havana, and I take it your family background was different from that of Generals Choy and Chui. Is this right?

MOISÉS SÍO WONG: Yes. My father arrived in Cuba in 1895.

---

forces. The Rebel Army fighters, who numbered 300 in late May, when the offensive began, with only 200 usable rifles, withstood, and by late July crushed, this effort. For accounts of this period, see Guevara, *Episodes of the Cuban Revolutionary War*, "From Batista's Final Offensive to the Battle of Santa Clara," and Hart, *Aldabonazo: Inside the Cuban Revolutionary Underground*, pp. 240–43.

7.   From January 2 to January 8, 1959, Fidel Castro led victorious Rebel Army columns from the Sierra Maestra to Havana, known as the Liberty Caravan. Mass rallies in support of the revolution and addressed by Castro greeted the caravan as it arrived in cities and towns across the island.

He came from China with his first wife. He had his first child in China—that is, my oldest brother. My father left my brother there with the boy's grandmother, and he came here to Cuba with his wife.

WATERS: In what circumstances?

SÍO WONG: He simply got the money together, bought the ticket, and came. He settled in Matanzas province, where there was a big Chinese community. He had a little grocery store in a small village in the countryside called San Pedro de Mayabón, in Los Árabos municipality.

My father had five children with his first wife. One in China and four here. His wife died, leaving him a widower. Among the peasants it was common to say, "Send the man a wife." So he sent off for another one, who was to be my mother. She was fifteen when she arrived. At the time, my father's children were fourteen, thirteen, twelve, and eleven. So my mother was only a year older than the eldest child she was caring for.

My mother should have gotten a medal. A heroine. She bore him nine children. In addition, she cared for four of the five children by my father's first marriage. When I was born in 1938, there were already eleven children in the household. I was number twelve.

During the first years of my life, we lived in San Pedro de Mayabón. It was a very small village, mostly peasants. I didn't go to school, but I did learn to read and write at home. My older sister Angelita, who'd attended school, taught me. I also learned arithmetic there—addition and subtraction.

At home we mainly spoke Chinese. But I learned Spanish too. Because even though I didn't go to a Cuban school at the time, many of the children I related to were not Chinese. As I grew older, I began forgetting Chinese, since I didn't use it much.

In 1947, when I was nine, my father suffered a stroke and became an invalid. The family moved here to Havana to better care for him.

My brother-in-law, who was Chinese, was very rich. He and my sister Isabel married in 1942 or 1943. I remember the huge wedding they had. I'd never seen anything like it. Chinese from all over Cuba came. Big trucks from Havana loaded down with beer, cake, sweets, and other delicacies. The wedding cake had seven layers. I was only a child, but I still remember that. This gentleman—my sister's husband—was the secretary of the Kuomintang in Cuba, the Chinese Nationalist Party, Chiang Kai-shek's party. He was a big businessman, with lots of money.

My brother-in-law opened a restaurant here in Havana, on San Lázaro and Crespo streets, a bar-restaurant where all my brothers and sisters worked. We got paid practically nothing.

At the time the minimum wage was 60 pesos a month. My brother later told me how my brother-in-law cooked the books to make it appear we were being paid 60 pesos. But he'd pay the oldest ones 45 at most. Sometimes even 30. And he didn't pay the children anything. He'd give us 20 centavos to go to the movies on Sunday. That was it.

I used to think my brother owned the bar, but it was my brother-in-law's and he was exploiting the entire family.

I found this out after returning from the revolutionary war. "Benito's been exploiting us," I told my mother.

"No," she replied. "We should thank him for putting up the money, setting up the business, and giving us work."

That was one way of looking at it, right? That he helped out our family by setting up the business. The other view—my view—was that we were being exploited. My brothers and sisters did the work and he got the profits. But I didn't fully understand "the exploitation of man by man" until after the triumph of the revolution.

After we came to Havana, I completed elementary school in two years. I already knew how to read and write. They gave me a test and put me in third grade. During summer vacation my sister got me a tutor and I jumped ahead to sixth grade. During other vacations the same tutor coached me, and I passed an exam to enter high school. That's how I completed elementary school in two years. We had to change my birth certificate to make me a year older, since you had to be twelve to get into high school and I was only eleven.

I spent a year in a private school, and then in 1951 I began attending Institute of Secondary Studies Number 1 in Havana. That's where I was when Batista carried out his coup on March 10, 1952.

Joining the revolutionary movement

KOPPEL: How did you come to join the revolutionary movement?

SÍO WONG: In Cuba students have always been in the vanguard of revolutionary struggles. On March 10 students at the University of Havana, led by young people like Fidel Castro and José Antonio Echeverría, protested strongly against the coup. That's how the struggle against the dictatorship began.

There was a strong student movement at the Institute of Secondary Studies, which had close ties to students at the University of Havana. A group of students at the high school quickly won me over. I didn't know anything about politics. I was very young. But it was there, as a student, that I began to express my feelings of discontent. Together with some other young people, we became active in the student struggle.

We began participating in demonstrations against the dictatorship together with students at the University of Havana. After the Moncada attack of July 26, 1953, these ties got even closer.

Historically, the University of Havana had played a prominent role in the struggles for independence, as well as during the 1933 revolution.[8] Fidel and many other leaders came out of the battles at the university.

Prior to July 26 we had ties to the left wing of the Orthodox Party—which is what Fidel belonged to at the time. That's where I got to know a group of revolutionaries that included Ñico López and Enio Leyva, and where I was recruited.

A group of us young people who lived in the Punta neighborhood organized a series of talks that we called "civic talks." Ñico López, who later participated in the Moncada assault and was killed following the *Granma* landing, would give them. Ñico was a worker, tall and skinny, very poor and modest. The talks presented a revolutionary political perspective. They were held at the Orthodox Party office, at 109 Prado, on the tree-lined promenade in Havana. As I said, the July 26 Movement didn't yet exist. At that time there was a left-wing group in the Orthodox Party led by Fidel and some young people, including Ñico López, Juan Manuel Márquez, Enio Leyva, and René Rodríguez.

After the attack on Moncada, the July 26 Movement was founded in 1955 and we joined it. Here in Havana the July 26 Movement Youth Brigades were formed, made up largely of students and young workers. They were headed by Gerardo Abreu (*Fontán*), an outstanding revolutionary with great organizational capability. He was an honest, straightforward, and selfless compañero who was black. The youth brigades devoted themselves primarily to propaganda, painting slogans

8.   See glossary, Revolution of 1933.

on walls, breaking display windows, throwing Molotov cocktails, small sabotage actions like that. Fontán named me head of the first youth brigade, created in the La Punta barrio.

By mid-1957 there was intense repression here in Havana, and it was decided I should go up to the Sierra Maestra. I headed off on July 4, Independence Day in the United States. I remember passing by a television on the street broadcasting a ceremony in which the U.S. national anthem was being played.

I first went to Bayamo and waited there a few months, from July to November, before I received authorization to go up. In the meantime, I was underground, pretending to be the nephew of a Chinese man who owned a laundry there.

Finally, at the end of November 1957, I joined Fidel's column.

Member of Rebel Army

WATERS: What happened when you got to the Sierra?

Sío Wong: The guerrilla unit was going through a critical juncture at that time.

The movement had gotten me a uniform, boots, a hammock, everything but a weapon. But I went up with three compañeros from Manzanillo—young peasants—who had nothing at all. They too were trying to join the Rebel Army, but they weren't bringing any food supplies or clothing.

I had a letter with me. It wasn't from Fontán, my immediate superior—he was the one I should have gotten a letter from. Instead, the letter was from one of the members of the *Granma* expedition. This compañero had come down from the mountains ill, and we had hidden him in a house. To us he was a god, a hero.

"Don't worry about a thing," the guy said. "I'll give you a letter to Fidel, and you won't have any problems." So he wrote me a letter of introduction to Fidel: "I send you Sío Wong, who's on the run owing to his revolutionary activities, and so on and so forth. Signed So-and-So." With that letter in hand, I thought I'd have no big problem.

It was difficult for me to make it up to the Sierra Maestra. I had been raised here in the city. I was a student. In addition, I was recovering from a fever, and I'd been very weak for three or four days. When I climbed the first hill, I fainted. The guide wanted to leave me behind but I told him, "If you leave me behind, I'm going to write to Fidel and they'll have you shot. You must take me up to the mountains."

So he borrowed a horse from a peasant woman, a widow who lived nearby. He put me on the horse, and that's how I reached the Sierra Maestra.

As we were arriving at Fidel's command post, I heard a compañero yell out, "Hey Fidel, even the Chinese are here!" That was my greeting.

They went inside a little house and gave Fidel my letter. I had always imagined that the compañeros would greet me with open arms.

"So, you're all on the run as a result of your work in the clandestine struggle?" Fidel said when he came out. "Where are you all from?"

The other guys said, "No, we're from somewhere different than he is, from Calicito. We've only burned a few canefields."

At that very moment Fidel had a platoon in the same area burning canefields. "So you're the ones who burned the Calicito canefields?" he said. "Then why do I have Captain Basante there with a platoon?"

I don't know, it's possible these guys really had burned some sugarcane. But Fidel did have a platoon in that area carrying out this specific mission, burning cane in that area.

Then he turned to me: "And you? So you're the one sent to

me by So-and-So?"

"Yes, commander."

"He obviously thinks he's a hero. He must be having the time of his life with the story of being part of the *Granma* expedition, instead of being here with us."

Then Fidel said, "Do you think this is an embassy? You do any little thing and then take sanctuary here? You didn't bring weapons, you didn't bring uniforms, you didn't bring boots, you didn't bring food, you didn't bring anything."

"Crescencio!" he yelled out. Crescencio Pérez, a peasant, was part of the rear guard. "Crescencio, lock them up for three days, with nothing but rice to eat."

As we were escorted to that part of the camp, I heard someone sitting on a rock say, "And if any of them try to escape, shoot 'em in the foot!" I later learned it was Raúl Castro.

The next day we were down at the river and Fidel came by. He apologized. "Please forgive me for the way I treated you yesterday, but this guy So-and-So really did a lousy thing. I gave him a direct order and he disobeyed. We face a critical situation with food, with clothes, with weapons. We don't have any weapons. If you want, you can all go back. When things get better, you can return."

"Commander, I can't go back to Havana," I said. "They're after me there."

The other three guys left, but I stayed. I remained in Column 1 led by Fidel and was eventually assigned to his command post. I remained there in La Plata until the Batista army's summer offensive began in 1958.

A clandestine mission

WATERS: While you were at the command post you were assigned a mission that required a clandestine trip back to Havana, right?

Sío Wong: Yes. At the end of January 1958, Fidel was preparing to send someone to go find Fontán—Gerardo Abreu—to get him out of Havana, where he was in imminent danger, and bring him to the Sierra. Since I was from Havana, compañero René Rodríguez, one of the *Granma* expeditionaries, suggested to Fidel that I go. That was right around the time of the second battle of Pino del Agua, and I was unable to leave right then. The battle occurred on February 4 or 5, and on February 7 news reached us that Fontán had been murdered.

Fontán was a leader of the July 26 Movement Youth Brigades, very courageous, with great integrity, an extraordinary compañero. He knew the entire organization in Havana, but Batista's men were unable to get him to reveal a single piece of information, even though they tortured him savagely.

For me the news was doubly painful, because Fontán had been my first leader inside the movement. He had always exemplified for me what a revolutionary is. Plus I knew Fidel had been planning to send me to get him.

A few days later, I was given the mission of going to Havana to find Sergio González, who we all knew as El Curita—"the little priest." He was head of action and sabotage here in the capital. He too was very much on the run.

During those days new columns led by Raúl Castro and Juan Almeida were being organized to leave the Sierra and open the Second and Third Fronts respectively. So it wasn't until March 10 that I could leave. I recall that I took advantage of Batista's celebrations of the anniversary of his coup to come down from the Sierra, go to Bayamo, make contacts, and then reach Havana.

I met El Curita in a park in the Víbora neighborhood of Havana at night, in front of the Mónaco movie theater. I'll never forget that meeting. I relayed Fidel's order to come back with me to the Sierra, since they were after him.

"Tell Fidel to forgive me for not obeying his order," Sergio González told me. "But as head of action and sabotage in such a complex situation, I can't go and abandon my men. I'm sure he'll understand. I'm grateful nevertheless for his concern for my safety."

There was no way he'd be convinced.

The meeting with Sergio González was on March 13, and I must have left Havana around March 14. When I informed Fidel that I had been unable to fulfill the mission, he was very sad, since he knew they were going to kill El Curita. And on March 19 they did. These were brave, proven, very valuable cadres who Fidel wanted to prevent from being killed.

Fidel knew the clandestine struggle in the city was very difficult. Fontán had been the victim of an informer. This person kept passing by, escorted by police in a patrol car, until he spotted Fontán in the street one day. That was how Fontán was nabbed.

I always give these cases as examples of how Fidel looked after the cadres, after the men, when he was leading a battle. He showed his concern for them and for having the fewest possible number of losses. But it's also an example of how these cadres assumed their responsibilities.

Fontán knew he was being hotly pursued. In fact, Fontán was the one who sent me to the Sierra. "They're close on your trail," he told me. "You have to go." Yet he himself remained in Havana. The same with El Curita, who also stayed here, despite an order from Fidel. It showed their sense of responsibility. That was true for many others, as well. Starting with Fidel. There's a letter to Fidel written by the combatants, asking him not to participate directly in combat. Because there was a period when he took a lot of risks.[9]

As far as I'm concerned, the most difficult struggle was the clandestine struggle in the city. In the city the enemy has all the advantages. Unlike the mountains, where the guerrilla has the advantage. He's the one who sets the ambushes. But in the city, the enemy has the advantage. And Havana was the most difficult place of all.

In Che's column

KOPPEL: You mentioned the Batista army's offensive in the Sierra Maestra during the summer of 1958. What were you doing during those months?

SÍO WONG: I was with Fidel during the first part of the offensive. He then sent me with a mine—an unexploded 100 lb. bomb dropped by an enemy plane, which we had converted into a mine—to hold back the enemy reinforcements that had landed to the south of the Sierra Maestra, near Palma Mocha. An elite enemy unit known as the Swift Battalion, under the command of Major Quevedo, was surrounded in El Jigüe, and Batista was sending reinforcements to break the siege. So Fidel sent me with a squad from Che's column to join Captain Ramón Paz's platoon.

In fact the enemy reinforcements didn't get there, since they were repulsed by Captain Andrés Cuevas's platoon in a decisive battle in which this courageous officer was killed.

I spent the rest of the offensive with that squad, participating in a number of battles, including the battle of El Jigüe, which was led personally by Fidel.[10] I also took part in the battle of

9. This letter can be found in Guevara, *Episodes of the Cuban Revolutionary War*, in the chapter "The Second Battle of Pino del Agua."

10. The battle of El Jigüe of July 11–21, 1958, was a decisive Rebel Army victory that sealed the defeat of the government's offensive in the

Casa de Piedra, Providencia, where Captain Paz was killed, and at Joval, where Commander René Ramos Latour (*Daniel*) died. When the offensive was over, I remained in Che's column.

In late August, Fidel designated Che and Camilo to organize two new columns. Che's column, "Ciro Redondo" Column 8, was to proceed toward the center of the country. Camilo's column, "Antonio Maceo" Column 2, had the mission of reaching Pinar del Río, the westernmost province.[11]

The choice of these two was a masterful decision by Fidel because of the qualities of both leaders. Che described Camilo as a tremendously creative combatant, a born guerrilla leader. The troops Camilo commanded had been in the plains of Bayamo, in Oriente, for several months, operating against the dictatorship's army. They had experience fighting in the plains. The rest of us had no experience fighting in the plains—all our combat had been in the mountains. Camilo's troops—the majority of the more than 90 combatants who set out—were veterans, with automatic weapons. That's why Camilo was given this mission.

As for Che's column of some 140 men, it was armed with weapons we had been able to assemble. The column included a group of officers and platoon and squad leaders who had served in the Sierra Maestra. But a large part of the column had just been through the School of Recruits in Minas del Frío.[12] They were green. They had no combat experience.

Sierra Maestra and was a turning point in the war.

11. In October Fidel Castro ordered Column 2 to remain in Las Villas province and operate in coordination with Column 8.

12. In April 1958 Che Guevara helped establish a Rebel Army school for recruits at Minas del Frío in the Sierra Maestra. Participants received military training, as well as literacy classes and political instruction.

I was in the forward detachment. Our platoon, which was made up of the most experienced combatants, had automatic weapons. I was in the second squad.

Before we left, Che got everyone together and explained the mission. Even if only a single combatant were left, Che said, he had to reach the destination and carry out the mission Fidel had given us.

I think Fidel chose Che to organize the struggle in the central part of the island for two reasons. First, because of the importance of that area. To be able to cut the dictatorship's forces in two. Second, because in Las Villas province there were troops from four different organizations: the July 26 Movement, Víctor Bordón's troops; the Revolutionary Directorate, which was the student group, led by Faure Chomón; the Popular Socialist Party, which had a unit in the northern part of the province led by Félix Torres; and the Second National Front of the Escambray, which had split from the Revolutionary Directorate and had ties to the Authentic Organization.

Fidel's objective was to unify these groups and cut the island in two. Because of his political abilities, Che was one of those capable of doing this. Che combined an outstanding mind with the qualities of a man of action. He was a combatant and a thinker.

The advance into central Cuba took place under very difficult conditions. It took us forty-five days to reach the Escambray. Eleven compañeros just couldn't keep up physically and left the unit halfway through the march. Some of them were murdered by the dictatorship.

Our feet were all chewed up not just from marching 500 kilometers, but also because we had to go through swamps, crossing the southern part of Camagüey province. It wasn't possible to use horses, cars, or anything else. We were on the move through very difficult conditions. In the mountains guerrillas have the advantage, but on the plains the enemy does, since he can move easily. And the enemy knew this terrain.

Whenever I felt I couldn't take any more, I'd look over at Che, who had used up the medication in his asthma inhaler. I'd see this Argentine guy with asthma who was willing to die for Cuba. If he could do it, how could I not do it? This gave me strength to keep going. I needed help from the other compañeros too, since sometimes I couldn't even lift my rifle, the lightweight M-1 carbine I was carrying. I'd grown up in the city and weighed less than 100 pounds.

Under these conditions we reached the Escambray in October 1958.

HAWKINS: What happened when you got there?

SÍO WONG: The first thing was that we bumped up against the forces of the Second National Front of the Escambray under the command of Jesús Carreras. We encountered a sign along the route into the mountains: "Troops from organizations other than the Second Front of the Escambray are not allowed here." It was signed by Carreras.

This organization had a provocative attitude, and they knew our column was coming.

Víctor Bordón had previously sent two officers to meet up with us. They'd guided us during the last part of the journey and had told us about the situation created by the Second Front.

Che succeeded in uniting the forces of the Revolutionary Directorate, the July 26 Movement, and the PSP. A pact was signed with the Directorate—the Pedrero Pact—in which their troops united under Che's command, combining their actions. A little later the PSP signed on too. The Second Front of the Escambray didn't sign the pact.

Virtually without rest after the long trip, Che attacked several small garrisons in the foothills of the mountains, such as Güinía de Miranda, Banao, and Caracusey.

Güinía de Miranda was the first battle after we arrived. We attacked a small army garrison of 40 men. We attacked around 5:00 AM and the battle had to end before dawn. Otherwise enemy planes would have gotten us.

On the march from the Sierra Maestra, we'd brought along a bazooka that had been seized during the army's summer offensive. But the compañero assigned didn't really know how to shoot it. So when the battle began, his first shot flew over the garrison. The second one fell short.

Che came over. "Hey chico, what are you doing?" Che grabbed the bazooka, stood in front of the garrison, and fired. The shot went straight through a window and into the building. They surrendered on the spot.

During the weeks that followed, Batista's army launched an offensive in the Escambray, which was repulsed, and our troops passed over to what became the final offensive.

One of the toughest battles occurred in Fomento, Choy's hometown. It was December 16, the first time we had assaulted an army garrison of that size in an urban area. We were attacked from the air during this three-day battle. After the enemy surrendered, we went on to liberate other cities including Cabaiguán, Placetas, Sancti Spíritus, Remedios, and Caibarién.

I remember an incident from the battle of Cabaiguán.

The forward platoon I was in, crossing through backyards, had managed to get right up to the enemy garrison, just across the street. I went to inform Che that we'd taken up this very advantageous position. To get there, you had to jump from a roof onto a wall, and then into a backyard. But it was 4:00 in the morning and dark. Che took a false step and fell, breaking his arm.

"What happened to the M-1?" Those were the first words out of Che's mouth. He's just broken his arm and he's asking about the rifle he was carrying!

The fighting culminated in the battle of Santa Clara. On January 1, 1959, we won that battle, Batista fled the island, and we headed for Havana.

I thought the war was over. I went through something similar to what López Cuba describes in *Making History*.[13] I'd left high school. I needed only two classes to get my diploma. So I went up to Che:

"OK, Che, the war's over. I want to become an electrical engineer."

"You're leaving *now*?" Che responded. "Don't be a jerk. Now the revolution begins."

WATERS: So you continued under Che's command?

Sío WONG: I was promoted to first lieutenant in early January 1959 and assigned to the military police, organized out of the La Cabaña fortress in Havana. That was Che's command post. The military police were in charge of overseeing military discipline. I also took night classes at the Institute of Secondary Studies. But I'd been out of school for four years and found it very hard to study. Plus, there were all the responsibilities of the Rebel Army.

Some months later Jorge Ricardo Masetti, an Argentine, set up Prensa Latina. Most members of the Rebel Army were peasants, but I'd been a student at the preuniversity level. Masetti knew this and tried to recruit me. "How would you like to be a journalist and help found a Latin American press agency?" he asked.

13. Mary-Alice Waters, ed., *Making History: Interviews with Four Generals of Cuba's Revolutionary Armed Forces* (Pathfinder, 1999), pp. 19–20.

I went to talk to Che.

"Che, Masetti is proposing I go work with him in Prensa Latina."

"I'll tell you this for the second time: Don't be a jerk. We need you in the army. Tell Masetti to go look for journalists somewhere else. You can't go."

That was another lesson.

The third time I got this type of lesson from Che was after he'd been named head of the National Bank. One of my sisters called and said her mother-in-law was dying in Macao, and she needed fifty dollars for a visa. She asked me to talk to Che.

So naively, I did.

"Che, my sister, whose mother-in-law is dying in Macao, needs fifty dollars to pay for a visa to go visit her."

Che stuck his hand in his pocket.

"All I have is 125 pesos." At the time, all officers got a wage of 125 pesos a month.

"If you need it, take it," he said. "But I don't have any dollars."

What a lesson! I've never forgotten it.

In my life as a revolutionary I've had a number of privileges. Most importantly for my revolutionary education, I served under three great leaders. First, Fidel in the Sierra Maestra. Second, as a combatant in Che's column. Third, beginning in 1965 I worked for nearly seven years directly with Raúl Castro, as aide to the minister of the Revolutionary Armed Forces. During this time I also had the privilege of working under Juan Almeida, who for a year and a half filled in as minister while Raúl was studying at the Military Academy.

That for me has been a great privilege. To have worked under leaders of that stature, to have known them, to have been under their command, and to learn from them.

Chinese in Cuba

WATERS: The three of you had quite different experiences growing up as Cubans of Chinese origin. Tell us a little about the Chinese emigration to Cuba. What place did it have in Cuba's history?

Sío Wong: The story begins in 1840, with the start of the first Opium War in China. Using opium imports as their main lever, the European colonial powers set out to dominate China. They had already introduced opium into the country in large amounts. Realizing the impact the growing opium trade was having on Chinese society and the Chinese people, the Manchu emperor issued a decree prohibiting its entry. The emperor sent a representative to Canton. A big operation was organized, destroying tens of thousands of chests of opium. The colonial powers, with England in the lead, used this as the pretext to go to war against China.

The Opium War ended in 1842, with China's defeat. Afterward, the colonial powers forced the Chinese rulers to make a number of concessions. First, China ceded Hong Kong to England and opened five ports to commerce—the ports of Canton (today Guangzhou), Amoy (today Xiamen), Fuzhou, Ningbo, and Shanghai. Over the next two decades China was forced to make more concessions, not just to the English but to other colonial powers too—the Americans, the French, the

Ports of origin of Chinese indentured laborers arriving in Cuba

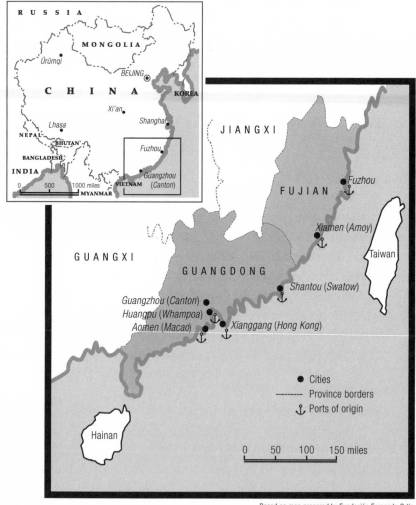

Based on map prepared by Fundación Fernando Ortiz

Portuguese, and so on. China opened different ports to them, from which they carried on their operations.

The English realized they could profit from dominating China in another way. They started to contract Chinese labor for exploitation in their colonies here in the Western Hemisphere: Trinidad and Tobago, Jamaica, Guyana, Barbados.

The Spanish Crown saw that this could be an alternative to African slaves, to develop the sugar industry here in Cuba above all.

Twenty-five years earlier, in 1817, England and Spain had signed a treaty abolishing the African slave trade. Spain didn't comply, of course, and continued bringing in slaves from Africa in violation of the treaty. In fact, more slaves were brought in than ever before. But since they couldn't do it as openly, they weren't able to bring in the amount of labor they needed.[14]

Another factor also influenced Spain's decision to bring in Chinese indentured labor. The 1841 census conducted by the Spanish indicated there were 1,017,000 people in Cuba, of whom only 418,000 were classified as white. There were 150,000 people in the category of free mestizos, and 432,000 slaves. That is, there were substantially more slaves and free men and women of mixed blood than there were whites.

There had already been a number of slave revolts. In 1844 there was a very famous case, the "Ladder Conspiracy," in which Plácido, a brilliant poet of mixed blood, was executed by firing squad. Some historians have said they don't know whether there really was such a conspiracy, or whether it was just a pretext by the Spanish authorities for repressive measures to try to forestall rebellions. But slave revolts were something they were very concerned about.

14. See glossary, Slavery in Cuba.

Taking their cue from the English, in 1844 the Spanish established a company in the port of Amoy to traffic in Chinese labor. They set up a barracks there. Amoy, or Xiamen, is right across from Taiwan, on the Straits of Taiwan.

The Chinese were contracted for a period of eight years. Pay was four pesos a month, plus food and clothing. They had to work for whoever bought or rebought their contract, which sold for seventy pesos. Thus they were indentured laborers. They were promised that after eight years they could choose to return to China or stay in the country as a free laborer. But they had no choice, of course. They had to stay since they didn't have money for the return passage.

The first shipment of contract laborers arrived in Cuba on June 3, 1847, aboard the Spanish brigantine ship *Oquendo*. Two hundred six arrived on that first ship. They disembarked at the port of Regla on Havana Bay, the same port the Spanish used for bringing in African slaves. They were put in barracks, and their contracts were sold to wealthy landowners, who treated them the same as they had slaves. On June 12 an English merchant ship, the *Duke of Argyle,* arrived with another 365 Chinese. A number had died during the journey, which took between four and five months. So these 500–600 in 1847 were the first Chinese to arrive.

Subsequently, partly in response to publicity about the mistreatment they had suffered, contracting was suspended by the Spanish Crown. But the queen authorized its resumption in 1852.

It's estimated that between 1848 and 1874, 141,000 Chinese were shipped out to Cuba, with 10–15 percent dying in passage. That's roughly the same number that went to the United States during those years. In proportion to population, however, emigration to Cuba was far more significant. In 1870 Cuba's population was 1.4 million; the population of the U.S. was 38 million.

These indentured laborers were put to work on sugar plantations and other agricultural estates. Conditions were very difficult. First of all, they didn't know the language. Second, they didn't know how to use a machete, how to cut cane. They didn't know how other tools were handled.

A large number of Chinese escaped to the hills, just as African slaves did. There were places known as "palenques," where runaway black slaves—*cimarrones*—went, and some Chinese did the same. Others committed suicide. They preferred suicide to continued mistreatment, to being treated as slaves.

In addition to direct emigration from China, between 1865 and 1875 some 5,000 Chinese made their way to Cuba from the United States. Many had built the railroads there. Recently I saw the movie *Wyatt Earp*, starring Kevin Costner. In it you see Chinese building the railroads across the United States. Well, many of these Chinese subsequently emigrated to Cuba, trying to escape the conditions they faced in the United States.

War of independence

On October 10, 1868, Cuba's War of Independence began.[15] Slaves were freed by the independence forces, and the contracts of all Chinese indentured laborers were declared null and void by the Republic in Arms.[16] Thousands of Africans and Chinese joined the struggle. There were battalions and companies composed entirely of Chinese.

On the corner of Línea and L streets in Havana, there's a monument to the Chinese who fought in the war of indepen-

15. See glossary, Cuban independence wars.

16. See glossary, Republic in Arms.

dence. On it is a plaque with a statement by General Gonzalo de Quesada, who was secretary of José Martí's Cuban Revolutionary Party. "There was not a single Chinese-Cuban deserter," Gonzalo de Quesada says. "There was not a single Chinese-Cuban traitor." Not a single case is known of any Chinese who helped the Spanish. Not one. Keep in mind that many native-born Cubans were part of the Volunteers, a notoriously brutal corps of Cubans who covered police duties so Spanish troops could fight the independence forces.

A number of years ago Fidel asked me if it's known how many Chinese participated in the 1868–98 independence wars. It hasn't been possible to determine, I said, since the Chinese used to change their names. They'd put down "Gustavo González" or "Ramón Fernández." They'd often take their masters' surname. Chinese names don't appear on the army rolls. Some historians estimate the number of Chinese combatants at 6,000. But no one knows for sure. It's possible there were more.

Then Fidel asked how many participated in the final war of liberation, that of 1957–59. How many sons of Chinese took part?

I told him we didn't know that either. Because unless the person's surname comes from the father, the next generation loses it. So there are many people whose Chinese ancestry can't be determined simply from looking at their names. Take, for instance, Esteban Lazo Hernández, ideological secretary of the party Central Committee; his grandfather was Chinese. Bárbara Castillo Cuestas, minister of domestic trade; her grandmother was Chinese. Lázaro Barredo, vice president of the International Relations Commission of the National Assembly; he too had Chinese grandparents. These Cuban leaders are all examples of people of Chinese ancestry. But they've lost their Chinese surnames.

CHOY: To give you an idea of the scope of Chinese participation in the war, in the battle of Las Guásimas alone, in 1874, there was a battalion of 500 native-born Chinese who fought under the command of General Máximo Gómez. An entire battalion.

SÍO WONG: In addition to being combatants, Chinese helped in other ways, such as contributing food.

My father, for example, had a little store in Matanzas during the 1895–98 war. One day he was upbraided by the colonial authorities for giving out some items from his store free of charge to a group of *mambises* who were passing by.[17]

"Why didn't you charge them?" he was asked.

"Well, the Spaniards pass by too and take things," was the excuse he gave. "And they don't pay either."

That's an example.

Many Chinese in the cities also contributed by providing information. To the Spanish colonial authorities, all Chinese looked the same. So Chinese would pass undetected when they went to the towns and cities to find out information about the Spanish troops. If anyone questioned them, they'd just say, "I no understand, I no understand."

WATERS: Did most of the Chinese in Cuba still speak mainly Chinese at that time? Or had they begun to speak Spanish? Or both?

SÍO WONG: The Chinese came here not knowing Spanish. Later they began learning a few words, but during the war communication was very difficult. That's why they were organized in separate companies or battalions.

There's an anecdote about an officer named Colonel Hernández serving under General Ignacio Agramonte. Hernández commanded a Chinese battalion, and he'd had it up to

17. See glossary, *Mambí.*

here with them. Since the officer and the troops often didn't understand each other, there were acts of indiscipline. So the colonel asked to meet with Agramonte. As the colonel approached the tent, Agramonte already knew why he was coming.

"Colonel, you must be so proud of your battalion," the general said as soon as they got inside. "You must be so proud of that heroic battalion, and how they love you as their commander." Think of it! General Ignacio Agramonte starts lauding the Chinese, how they loved their commander, their heroic attitude in this battle and that battle, how good they were. The colonel undoubtedly didn't say a word about what he'd really come to talk about, which was to ask to be transferred, since he was tired of dealing with the Chinese troops.

There's a fact that also illustrates the extent of Chinese participation in our wars of independence.

In 1901, after the final independence war was over, a constitution was approved. It included a provision—Article 65—that any foreigner who had fought for ten years for Cuba's freedom, arms in hand, would be considered Cuban by birth. He could even be president of the republic. That provision was put in for Máximo Gómez, who had commanded the army and was Dominican. But Máximo Gómez didn't accept the proposal. He said no, he was Dominican, a foreigner. A foreigner! Imagine!

Only four individuals qualified under that special constitutional provision: General Máximo Gómez, who was Dominican; General Carlos Roloff, who was Polish; and two Chinese—Lieutenant Colonel José Bu and Captain José Tolón (Lai Wa). They had fought in the three wars. Some historians suggest that Rius Rivera, who was Puerto Rican, also qualified, but that remains a disputed question. Anyway, these examples speak to the participation of Chinese in

Chinese fighters in Cuba's 1868–78 independence war.

Biblioteca Nacional José Martí

the independence wars.

KOPPEL: When did the system of contract labor end?

SÍO WONG: "Good treatment" for Chinese, "as religion and humanity demand," was recommended in a Royal Order by Queen Isabel II in 1847. The order also suggested that Chinese and blacks be kept apart.

In 1857 the Royal Council put a cap on the number of Chinese allowed to enter Cuba. And in 1860, owing to pressures from other foreign powers in China, Spain had to agree to prohibit sending Chinese contract labor to the American continent. Despite this, Chinese contract laborers in fact continued to be brought in until 1874.

During Cuba's independence war, the Spanish crown became alarmed at the Chinese role in the independence army. So in 1871 the crown issued another Royal Decree. It stated that based on "the difficulties" and "grave damage" caused by immigrants breaking "their commitments," Chinese laborers were endangering "public order" and aiding "the enemies of the nation." Therefore, "in the interests of tranquility," the bringing of Chinese contract laborers into Cuba was suspended.

On November 17, 1877, the Peking Agreement was signed by China and Spain, ending the criminal trade of indentured Chinese labor in Cuba. But Cuba itself was not informed about this until June 29, 1879, when it was published in the *Gaceta de La Habana*.

Creation of Chinese community

HAWKINS: How did the Chinese barrios in Havana and elsewhere in Cuba develop?

SÍO WONG: As Chinese completed their eight-year contracts and were set free, most stayed alive by becoming street vendors. They sold fruits, fried foods, vegetables, and other things. These vendors founded the first Chinese barrios. There were a few small restaurants and stands on the corner of Zanja and Rayo streets in Havana. A Chinese district gradually grew up around there, where people spoke both Chinese and Spanish. Several Chinese-language newspapers were established. In 1867 members of the Chinese community formed the first Chinese society, the Kit Yi Tong.

Eventually the Chinese district in Havana came to be the most important Chinatown in Latin America. Perhaps surpassed in the Americas only by San Francisco.

WATERS: What was the geographic spread of the Chinese population?

Sío Wong: Initially the Chinese were concentrated in the provinces where the sugar industry was most highly developed, such as Havana, Matanzas, Villa Clara, and Oriente. But later on they spread to all the provinces and cities.[18]

Most Chinese became merchants and traders. Food services, laundries, services of that type. If you didn't make it in Las Tunas, you went to Camagüey, or someplace else. Like Chui's father did. Through this process the Chinese spread throughout the country.

WATERS: Virtually all the Chinese who came as indentured laborers were men—I've read that in some years it was over 99 percent. That must have had a big impact on the development of the Chinese community.

Sío Wong: That's clearly one reason there was a lot of intermarriage. Many Chinese men married Cuban women. Among the Chinese there weren't the same pressures against intermarriage you see in some other communities—the Jewish community, for example.

There's an interesting case in my own family. We were

18. See map showing spread of Chinese population in Cuba on p. 11.

Chinese barrio in Havana, late 19th century.

fourteen brothers and sisters—six girls and eight boys. My mother insisted that all the girls had to marry men both of whose parents were Chinese. None of them could marry the son of a Chinese and a Cuban; he had to be the son of a Chinese man and a Chinese woman. So that's what happened. And all us boys married Cuban girls.

WATERS: What was the scope of the Chinese emigration to Cuba after 1874, when the system of contract labor was effectively ended?

Sío WONG: It was reduced. But because of the prevailing conditions in China—a backward, semicolonial country in which landlords, warlords, and foreign imperialists criminally exploited millions of peasants and workers—many Chinese, in desperation, emigrated to a number of countries, including Cuba, in search of better conditions of life.

Discrimination against Chinese

WATERS: What types of discrimination and racism did the Chinese face?

CHUI: There were many things. For example, I remember the taunt, "Chino Manila pa' Canton." People would see us and they'd shout that. In effect, "Chinaman from Manila, go back to Canton!" You remember that, don't you, Sío?

Sío WONG: Oh yes.

CHUI: That's how we were viewed by some people.

KOPPEL: Why did they shout "Chino Manila"? What was that about?

Sío WONG: Some contract laborers arrived by way of the Philippines, which was then a Spanish colony too. "Chinaman from Manila" was a derogatory expression for all Chinese.

CHUI: I also remember how they used to yell, "Narra, hey narra!"

Sío WONG: Calling a Chinese person in Cuba "narra" is

like saying "nigger" to a black person in the United States. In Cuba the comparable slur for blacks was "niche." Blacks were called "niche" and Chinese were called "narra." "Hey, narra!" It was an offensive, insulting word, like "slant-eye" or "chink."

There was discrimination against blacks. And there was discrimination against Chinese. There were places neither could go. The racial discrimination took economic forms too.

WATERS: For example?

SÍO WONG: Access to education, for instance. There were private schools and private universities they couldn't attend. And there were private clinics they were barred from, where health care was better than what was available to the poor.

CHUI: There were elite clubs, too. Take the case of the owner of the Rosita Hotel, for example. He was a millionaire but he was mulatto—and they wouldn't let him into one of the major clubs. This same man, under Batista, built a social club—Club Alfonso—for mulattos and blacks, but later they wouldn't let blacks in. Only mulattos, provided they didn't look too mulatto!

SÍO WONG: There were elite places where you didn't see blacks. And Chinese couldn't go either. There were beaches like Tarará outside Havana, for example, where Chinese and blacks—or any poor person—couldn't go. Or Brisas del Mar, east of Havana. This was a private beach, and they wouldn't let you in.

In the Miramar section of Havana, there was a special private police force paid for by the rich. At night they'd patrol the streets, demanding, "Where's your identification? What are you doing around here?"

Blacks were the main target of that kind of discrimination. In Santa Clara, for example, there was a promenade in the park for whites and a different promenade for blacks. Chinese were allowed to use the promenade for whites. But the Chinese were discriminated against in many ways too. Choy told how they wouldn't let his friend into a dance with his girlfriend because it was for whites only.

So there was discrimination against blacks and Chinese. There was also discrimination because of sex. There was discrimination against the poor.

Class divisions in Chinese community

WATERS: What was the class structure of the Chinese population?

SÍO WONG: They were shopkeepers primarily. But the Chinese community was far from homogeneous. It was divided between rich and poor. There were very rich merchants and businessmen who were quite powerful economically. There was a Chinese-owned bank. There was a Chinese Chamber of Commerce. There were Chinese millionaires.

There was one millionaire who built a house by the Almendares River that is now the Pavo Real Restaurant. It's an exact replica of a house in Hong Kong, on the banks of the Pearl River, which belonged to the man's father. So he sent for the architects, they duplicated it exactly, and we have that house.

Then there were the poorest Chinese, the street vendors, and so forth.

One can talk of discrimination—we Chinese were discriminated against racially because we were Chinese. But I would say that the economic discrimination by the rich against the poor was greater.

WATERS: Over the first sixty years of the twentieth century, after what's known in the United States as the Spanish-American War, Washington was the dominant imperialist power in Cuba. How did that affect the Chinese community?

SÍO WONG: The U.S. government had a great deal of influence

on the Cuban government during those decades. We were a nominally independent republic, with a capitalist system. The U.S. ambassador dictated policy. Sumner Welles, Franklin D. Roosevelt's ambassador in the 1930s, was infamous for imposing Washington's interests, for example. The U.S. military mission had great influence on the Cuban army.

Washington's domination was reflected in the weight the U.S.-backed Chiang Kai-shek dictatorship had in the Chinese community here. Chiang Kai-shek led the counterrevolutionary forces that fled to Taiwan after they were overthrown by the Chinese Revolution of 1949. His party, the Kuomintang, or Nationalist Party, was led in Cuba by a group of wealthy merchants and had considerable influence among the Chinese population. Before 1959, for example, the Chung Wah Casino[19]—an umbrella group of all the Chinese societies—was under the influence of the Kuomintang.

After 1949 the Cuban government had diplomatic relations with Taiwan, not Beijing, and that Chinese consulate played a role in the Chinese community. Its office was next to the office of the president of the Chung Wah Casino in Havana.

As I said, the Chinese population here was divided between rich and poor. Among the rich, the impact of U.S. domination and influence was not much different from what it was for the Cuban oligarchy as a whole.

With the triumph of the revolution in 1959 there was a polarization in the Chinese community similar to the rest of society. The wealthy Chinese merchants and businessmen, as well as some of the smaller Chinese merchants, abandoned the country. The majority of the Chinese, however, joined the revolution. The Kuomintang Society, which had been affiliated to the Kuomintang Party in Taiwan, became the Socialist

19. The word *casino* in Spanish usually means society, or club.

Alliance, and the leadership of the Chung Wah Casino was taken over by revolutionaries. In 1960 Cuba cut its ties with Taiwan and formally recognized the People's Republic of China, the first country in Latin America to do so.

WATERS: Where did the Chinese who left Cuba go?

SÍO WONG: Some to Taiwan. Many to the United States, Canada, Central America, and to other countries.

WATERS: In New York there are still many Chinese-Cuban restaurants, which were established soon after 1959.

SÍO WONG: There's a funny story about that. In 1988 the agreement ending the war in Angola and granting independence to Namibia was signed at the United Nations in New York City.[20] A group of Cuban generals who had participated in the defense of Angola against the South African invasion went to New York for the signing.[21]

One day some of them wanted to eat Chinese food, and a compañero from the Cuban Mission to the United Nations took them to a restaurant in Chinatown. When they got there, a number of compañeros, using their poor English, tried to order food. But they were having great difficulty.

After a while the guy in the restaurant stopped them and said in fluent Spanish, "Save your effort, fellas, I'm Cuban."

After 1959

HAWKINS: What's the most important measure taken after 1959 to eliminate discrimination against Chinese and blacks?

SÍO WONG: The principal measure was the revolution it-

---

20. See part 2.

21. The six Cuban generals in New York for the signing were Abelardo Colomé, Leopoldo Cintra Frías, Ramón Espinosa, Víctor Schueg, Rafael Moracén, and Pascual Martínez Gil.

self. It was no single action, although a number of measures were very important. Like banning discrimination in hiring. And turning all beaches into public property, open to everybody.[22]

But the socialist revolution was made precisely to eliminate inequalities. To bring about social justice. To end discrimination against blacks, women, and the poor. To close the gulf between rich and poor.

KOPPEL: I've heard that a Chinese-Cuban militia unit helped carry out the nationalizations of the big capitalist holdings in 1960 and was instrumental during the early years of the revolution in eliminating drugs, prostitution, and gambling from Havana's Chinatown. Is that true?

SÍO WONG: That was the José Wong Brigade, which was part of the Revolutionary National Militia. It was formed in early 1960. José Wong was a member of the Chinese Communist Party who came to Cuba around 1927, fleeing Kuomintang repression in Canton after the revolutionary process there had been crushed. He became a revolutionary fighter against the Machado dictatorship here in Cuba, along with Julio Antonio Mella and Rafael Trejo. In 1930 he was taken prisoner and assassinated in Havana's Príncipe Prison.

Militia units were formed by the Cuban people everywhere during the revolution's first days. There were student militias at the university, workers militias in the factories, peasant militias in the countryside. In my neighborhood of San Lázaro, for example, we created a militia named after Pepe Valladares, a martyr from there killed in the struggle against Batista. By

22. On March 22, 1959, in what became known as the "Proclamation against Racism," Prime Minister Fidel Castro presented the initial measures being taken by the revolutionary government to ban racial discrimination in Cuba. A translation of the speech was published in the *Militant*, April 19, 1999.

late 1959, with the number of new militia units still increasing, they began to unify into a single body, the Revolutionary
National Militia.

The José Wong Brigade, which did the things you mentioned, also participated in defeating the mercenary invasion
at Playa Girón in 1961.[23]

KOPPEL: What's the situation of the Chinese community in
Cuba today?

SÍO WONG: There are now only about 300 Chinese in Cuba
who were born in China. There has been no significant immigration since the revolution in 1959, so the remaining Cubans
born in China are all elderly.

Chinese societies like the Chung Wah Casino have tried
to rescue the cultural traditions of the Chinese community.
But it's been difficult, since nearly all the children of Chinese
are fully integrated into Cuban society. We've tried to bring
them together, but undoubtedly it's not the same as in other
countries. The societies that exist have forty or fifty members,
and they've had to be opened up to third-, fourth-, fifth-, even
sixth-generation Chinese to make the societies a little bigger.
But they survive. You can see them in Havana's Chinatown.

WATERS: One of the projects of the Cuba-China Friendship
Association, which you're the president of, is the restoration
of Havana's Chinatown. Is that something recent?

SÍO WONG: In 1993 a group of Chinese descendents approached the Cuba-China Friendship Association, solicit-
ing its support for a restoration project for Chinatown. Out
of this came the Chinatown Promotional Group. The project
has two main aims. One is preserving the traditions, art, and
culture of Chinese in Cuba. The other is to revitalize the Chinese barrio in Havana economically and commercially.

23. See glossary, Playa Girón.

From the cultural point of view, we've registered significant advances. The Chinese House of Arts and Traditions holds exhibits and literary competitions, as well as contests in the visual arts, dance, music, theater. It even offers instruction in the Chinese language.

The project to rescue Chinatown has also received support from various Chinese societies across the island, including the Chung Wah Casino, the principal center of the Chinese community here.

The embassy of the People's Republic of China has given its support, too. For example, the archway at the entrance to Chinatown was donated by Chinese deputy prime minister Li Langqing.

Currently the Promotional Group functions under the office of the official historian of the City of Havana, compañero Eusebio Leal. That's the office responsible for the enormous project to restore Old Havana, and they're in the best position to move this ambitious project forward too. But the Cuba-China Friendship Association will continue giving all its support.

Cuba's example

WATERS: There are Chinese minorities in other countries of Latin America, as well as the United States. But the conditions they live and work under are very different from those in Cuba today. How do you see the changes that have taken place in your lifetime?

Sío WONG: In 1999 there was an international conference on the Chinese diaspora held in Cuba. There's an association of the Chinese diaspora in every country. The organization's president lives in Singapore. The event here was sponsored by the University of Havana, and representatives of Chinese communities in various countries participated. Many came from the United States, from Canada, from Southeast Asia.

I recall that the president and his wife asked me, "How is it possible that you, a descendent of Chinese, occupy a high government post, are a deputy in the National Assembly, and a general of the Armed Forces? How is that possible?"

The answer doesn't lie in the degree of Chinese participation in the war of independence. That is worth studying, since nothing similar happened in any other country where Chinese indentured workers were taken. But here too, before the triumph of the revolution, we Chinese were discriminated against.

What's the difference in the experience of Chinese in Cuba and other countries of the diaspora? The difference is that here a socialist revolution took place. The revolution eliminated discrimination based on the color of a person's skin. Above all, it eliminated the property relations that create not only economic but also social inequality between rich and poor.

That's what made it possible for the son of Chinese immigrants to become a government representative, or anything else. Here discrimination—against blacks, against Chinese, against women, against the poor—was ended. Cubans of Chinese descent are integrated.

To historians and others who want to study the question, I say that you have to understand that the Chinese community here in Cuba is different from Peru, Brazil, Argentina, or Canada.

And that difference is the triumph of a socialist revolution.

PART II

STRENGTHENING THE REVOLUTION

Cuban internationalist volunteers in Angola, February 1990. The troops are preparing their withdrawal at the end of a 16-year mission that successfully defended Angola from South African invasion and helped bring about the fall of the white supremacist apartheid system.

Cuba's internationalist mission to Angola, 1975–91

Between November 1975 and May 1991, more than 375,000 Cuban volunteers responded to a request for solidarity from the government of Angola. The volunteer combatants took part in an internationalist mission to defend Angola against imperialist-inspired attempts by Zaire to annex oil-rich Cabinda province and against two major invasions by the South African armed forces, as well as the apartheid regime's ongoing military operations in alliance with U.S.-backed counterrevolutionary groups.

The first Cuban troops arrived only days before Angola was to become independent from Portugal on November 11, 1975. The allies of the invading South African troops, with U.S. support, were already closing in on the capital city of Luanda.

"When the Angolan people were about to attain independence, imperialism worked out a way to crush the revolutionary movement in Angola," Fidel Castro explained on December 22, 1975, in his first public announcement of the Angola operation. "They planned to take hold of Cabinda, with its oil, before November 11; to seize Luanda before November 11. And to carry out this scheme, the U.S. government launched South African troops against Angola.... It was a solid plan; the only thing was that the plan failed.... They had not counted on international solidarity," including "the support we Cubans gave Angola."

As early as the spring of 1975, Castro explained in the same speech, U.S. imperialism was already investing tens of millions of dollars "to supply arms and instructors to the counterrevolutionary, secessionist Angolan groups." In the summer of that year, at Washington's instigation, troops from Zaire entered Angolan territory, and in August South African forces occupied the area around the Cunene River in the south. "At that time there wasn't a single Cuban instructor in Angola," Castro said. Cuba's first material aid and instructors were sent in early October at the request of the Angolan government when the country "was being openly invaded by foreign forces. However, no Cuban military unit had been sent to Angola to participate directly in the fight, nor was that projected."

By early November, the situation faced by the Angolan people had become critical. Cuba's decision to respond to an appeal for combat forces is described in an account of the operation by Colombian writer Gabriel García Márquez based on extensive interviews with Cuban leaders: "The leadership of the Communist Party of Cuba did not have more than twenty-four hours to make the decision, and it did so, without vacillation, on November 5.... That decision was an independent and sovereign act of Cuba and it was only after it was taken, and not before, that the Soviet Union was notified." The mission was named Operation Carlota, after a slave woman from the Triunvirato sugar mill in Matanzas, Cuba, who, armed with a machete, led a slave rebellion in 1843 that extended over a number of plantations in that province. Known as "Black Carlota," she was captured and drawn and quartered.

The Cuban internationalists were decisive in repelling the invading forces a few kilometers outside Luanda. By March 27, 1976, "when the last South African soldiers crossed the Namibian border after a retreat of more than 700 kilometers, one of the most brilliant pages in the liberation of Black Africa had been written," said Fidel Castro on April 19, 1976.

Thousands in Cuba volunteered to be part of this effort. "The immense majority went to Angola in the full conviction that they were carrying out an act of political solidarity, with the same consciousness and courage with which fifteen years earlier they had defeated the invasion at Playa Girón," García Márquez wrote. "That is why Operation Carlota was not a simple expedition of professional soldiers, but a popular war."

In sending Cuban troops, Castro pointed out on July 26, 1976, "we are not doing a favor but simply fulfilling a duty." A people "that is not willing to fight for the freedom of others will never be ready to fight for its own."

After being driven back across the border, the apartheid regime in South Africa, with the support and aid of the U.S. government, helped initiate a bloody counterrevolutionary war against the new Angolan government waged by UNITA (National Union for the Total Independence of Angola). Faced with this situation, Angola requested that Cuba maintain its internationalist mission. The war turned into a stalemate lasting more than a decade, during which hundreds of thousands of Angolans were killed.

Toward the end of 1987, in an attempt to break the impasse, the Angolan government—following the guidance of the Soviet military personnel aiding them, and against the advice of the Cuban leadership—undertook an ill-conceived offensive against UNITA forces holding the southeastern provinces of the country. With Angola's army overextended, the apartheid regime saw an opportunity to trap and annihilate the best Angolan units, thereby decisively shifting the balance of forces in the war. It sent in large numbers of South African troops, tanks, and planes, which rapidly advanced hundreds of miles into Angola, creating a critical situation.

In response, the Cuban revolutionary leadership decided to massively reinforce Cuba's military mission, and to do so rapidly. As Castro later explained on December 5, 1988, "In this action

Angola, November 1987–April 1988

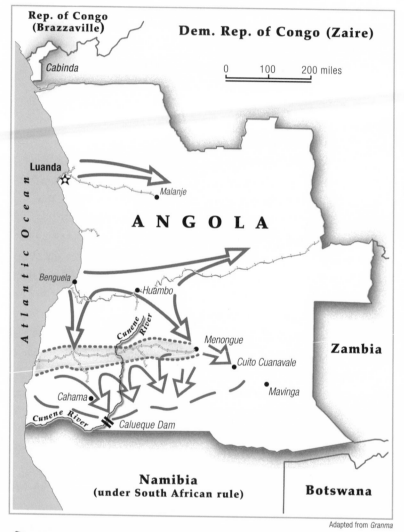

Rep. of Congo (Brazzaville)

Dem. Rep. of Congo (Zaire)

Cabinda

0   100   200 miles

Luanda

Atlantic Ocean

Malanje

A N G O L A

Benguela

Huambo

Cunene River

Menongue

Cuito Cuanavale

Zambia

Cahama

Cunene River

Mavinga

Calueque Dam

Namibia
(under South African rule)

Botswana

Adapted from *Granma*

Arrows denote movement of Cuban-Angolan-SWAPO forces.

Cuban troop positions, November 1987.

Forward position of Cuban-Angolan-SWAPO troops, April 1988.

the revolution staked everything, it staked its own existence, it risked a huge battle against one of the strongest powers located within the Third World, against one of the richest powers, with significant industrial and technological development, armed to the teeth, at such a great distance from our small country and with our own resources, our own arms. We even ran the risk of weakening our defenses, and we did so."

The key position standing in the way of a final breakthrough for the South African forces was the town of Cuito Cuanavale in southern Angola, where a group of Angolan and Cuban troops were surrounded. The town's defenders, led by the Cubans, repulsed repeated South African thrusts over several months, while reinforced Cuban and Angolan forces moved toward Cuito Cuanavale and others mounted a flanking operation in a broad arc southward toward the Namibian border. By March 1988 South African positions were being threatened, and the apartheid forces realized they could not take Cuito Cuanavale. The retreat began. An account of this operation and its place in the African liberation struggle can be found in the speeches by Fidel Castro and Nelson Mandela in the appendix on pp. 169–86.

The South Africans sued for peace. In December 1988 an agreement was signed at the United Nations in New York between Angola, Cuba, and South Africa, in the presence of representatives of the U.S. government. The accords called on South Africa to withdraw its forces from Angola and to grant independence to Namibia. Immediately following the signing of this agreement, Cuba and Angola jointly agreed to the withdrawal of Cuban forces. The last Cuban troops left Angola in May 1991; some 2,000 Cuban internationalists had died in the nearly sixteen-year mission.

"The crushing defeat of the racist army at Cuito Cuanavale was a victory for the whole of Africa!" said Nelson Mandela during a visit to Cuba in 1991. "Cuito Cuanavale has been a turning point in the struggle to free the continent and our country from the scourge of apartheid!"[24]

■

WATERS: At various times between 1975 and 1991 all three of you served in Angola. Can you tell us a little more about this internationalist mission?

CHUI: The Cuban Revolution has been true to the legacy of the internationalists who helped us in the war for independence and in other struggles since then. Generals Máximo Gómez, who was Dominican; Carlos Roloff, who was Polish; Luis Marcano, who was Dominican; Juan Rius Rivera, who was Puerto Rican—all fought for Cuba's independence.

CHOY: Henry Reeve, "El Inglesito."

CHUI: Yes, the "Little Englishman" who was actually American.

CHOY: And Thomas Jordan, another American, who had fought in the U.S. Civil War on the side of the Confederacy.

CHUI: Throughout our history there were many internationalists who fought for our freedom. We have been true to their legacy.

24. The 1975 and 1976 speeches by Castro that tell the story of the initial chapter of the internationalist mission in Angola are contained in *Fidel Castro Speeches: Cuba's Internationalist Foreign Policy, 1975–80* (Pathfinder, 1981). That book also includes "Cuba in Angola: Operation Carlota" by Gabriel García Márquez. Castro's December 1988 speech on the battle of Cuito Cuanavale, excerpted in the appendix to this book, is printed in *In Defense of Socialism: Four Speeches on the 30th Anniversary of the Cuban Revolution* (Pathfinder, 1989). Mandela and Castro's speeches from 1991, also excerpted in the appendix, are contained in *How Far We Slaves Have Come! Cuba and South Africa in Today's World* (Pathfinder, 1991).

When we carry out missions in countries that request our assistance, we have the opportunity to do what they did.

We lent assistance to the Congo, for example, and to the Republic of Guinea when Sékou Touré was president. At various times we also aided Guinea-Bissau, Cape Verde, Somalia, Ethiopia, Algeria, Syria, Yemen, Oman, Sierra Leone, São Tomé and Príncipe, Benin, Equatorial Guinea, and other nations in Africa and the Middle East.[25]

In terms of the Americas, there's Nicaragua, Grenada, and Guyana, among others, including Venezuela today.

We should stress that this aid has been of every type. It includes medical, construction, educational, and cultural assistance as well as military missions.

Sío Wong: Our people hold socialist and internationalist ideas. That's how we've been educated. What other country can provide four or five thousand doctors for voluntary internationalist work when asked for help? But not only doctors. Our soldiers. The 375,000 Cuban combatants who served in Angola between 1975 and 1991 were all volunteers. That may not be well known, but it's a fact.

Each one was asked: "Are you willing to participate?"

"No, my mother's sick," someone might answer.

"Then you don't go," he'd be told.

It was genuinely voluntary. This was one of the conditions established by the party and Fidel. How can you risk your life for a just cause unless it's voluntary? There's no other way it can be done.

25. The story of some of these early efforts is recounted in *Pasajes de la guerra revolucionaria: Congo* by Che Guevara (published in English as *The African Dream*, New York: Grove Press, 2000), *From the Escambray to the Congo* by Víctor Dreke (Pathfinder, 2002), and *Conflicting Missions: Havana, Washington, and Africa, 1959–1976* by Piero Gleijeses (Chapel Hill: University of North Carolina Press, 2002).

The battle of Cuito Cuanavale

WATERS: Nelson Mandela called the battle of Cuito Cuanavale in 1987–88 "a turning point in the history of Africa." Yet outside Cuba—and much of Africa—this battle is largely unknown.

Sío WONG: In late 1987 the enemy almost completely surrounded a group of Cuban and Angolan troops at Cuito Cuanavale. And the decisive battle took place there. The battle lasted more than four months, and in March 1988 the South African army was defeated. That defeat marked the beginning of the end. It forced them to sit down at the negotiating table. And they accepted an agreement.

Otherwise the offensive would have continued . . .

CHUI: . . . which could have endangered their stability.

Sío WONG: Yes. And their defeat had a whole series of consequences—including the independence of Namibia and the release of Mandela after twenty-seven years in prison.

CHUI: It "broke the back of the South African army," to use Fidel's words.

Sío WONG: How is it possible that the South Africans, with all their military and economic might, were forced to sit down at the negotiating table? From a strategic point of view, what we carried out was a deterrence operation. Our strategy was to concentrate a mass of tanks in southern Angola. How many tanks were there, Chui? Five hundred, a thousand? You'd have to look up the exact figures. It was a deterrent force, since it could have crossed into Namibia and continued southward.

The idea was always to do battle with the fewest possible casualties. How to accomplish that? Through superiority in the relationship of forces.

At one point in that operation our troop strength in Angola

The South African command calculated we would need at least six months to transport the personnel, arms, and combat equipment equivalent to one division. It took South African strategists longer to realize that, by doubling our total forces and increasing them many times over on the Southern Front, we had taken control of the air for the first time, after twelve years.

To achieve this, some real feats of labor were necessary, such as building the Cahama airport in only seventy days, putting vital enemy objectives within our reach. Moreover, on the southern front we deployed a strike force that consisted, among other things, of 998 tanks, more than 600 armored vehicles, and 1,600 artillery pieces, mortars, and antiaircraft defense equipment....

Cuito held out. All the South African attempts to advance were halted. Their sophisticated long-range artillery, which kept up the shelling day and night, did not frighten the Angolan-Cuban forces and turned out to be ineffective. Meanwhile, on the southwestern flank, a powerful group aided by SWAPO units was seriously threatening points of strategic importance to the enemy. The clashes with reconnoitering enemy detachments in Donguena and Tchipa, and the air strike on their positions in Calueque, convinced the South Africans that it was impossible to obtain a military victory.

—RAÚL CASTRO

At ceremony greeting the last returning Cuban internationalists from Angola, May 27, 1991

reached 50,000, equipped with artillery, tanks, and planes—80 percent of them deployed in the south. We built roads for our tanks and artillery. In two months we built an airstrip so our planes could provide cover for forces at the front, since the South Africans had a large number of aircraft. Up to that time, they had air superiority.

Leaders set the example

WATERS: Compañero Chui, what were your responsibilities related to the Angola campaign?

CHUI: Starting in September 1971 I was second in command of the 10th Directorate of the Revolutionary Armed Forces, the unit in charge of internationalist assistance. I served under Commander Raúl Díaz Argüelles, who had participated in Guinea-Bissau's war of liberation. In December 1975, barely a month after the start of our internationalist mission in Angola, Argüelles, who commanded our forces there, was killed by a mine, and I was named head of this directorate.

As Moisés mentioned earlier, I too had the honor of working under three leaders: Fidel, Raúl, and Almeida. I served under Almeida in the Sierra and am doing so again today in the Association of Combatants of the Cuban Revolution.

I served under Raúl in the Ministry of the Revolutionary Armed Forces from the time I was very young. He has educated and trained me. In the armed forces I was head of a number of bodies: Armaments, the 10th Directorate, and Cadres. I was also deputy chief of staff.

And beginning in September 1975, for two years I had the honor of working together with Fidel and Raúl in the Special Command Post to lead our forces during the first phase of the internationalist assistance to the people of Angola. The command post of Operation Carlota, as it was known, directed the dispatch and deployment of forces—first our instructors and then our combat volunteers—as well as supplies.

I acquired a lot of experience, not to mention Fidel's knocking some sense into me from time to time. But that's how you learn, and that's how leadership cadres are trained.

KOPPEL: When were you in Angola?

CHUI: I was there briefly in 1976, and I later served from 1986 to 1988. As Mary-Alice said, Moisés, Choy, and I all served in Angola.

But not only that. The majority of the officers of the armed forces at that time took part in internationalist missions to one or more African countries. We gained experience in combat, troop organization, transport, and logistics. At times we did so together with the Soviets.

In 1977 I participated in establishing Cuba's military mission in Ethiopia, and I was also part of similar undertakings in Mozambique in 1977 and Nicaragua in 1979.

In 1986 I was named deputy chief of staff of the Cuban military mission in Angola, a responsibility I held until December 1987. At that time, on my request, I was named head of Operation 31st Anniversary—the reinforcement of Cuban troops and munitions for the battle of Cuito Cuanavale, which had begun in November. That operation was organized and directed by the commander in chief.

SÍO WONG: I'll tell you a story that says something about Fidel's leadership of the Angola mission. In 1984 or 1985 Fidel went to the Soviet Union to attend the funeral of the Communist Party general secretary—I don't remember whether it was Andropov or Chernenko.[26] The room was filled with Soviet marshals and generals, who were wondering where Fidel had studied strategy, operational arts, military science. They had seen how Fidel directed the war in Angola and were astounded by it.

26. Soviet Communist Party general secretary Yuri Andropov died in February 1984. He was replaced by Konstantin Chernenko, who died in March 1985.

To organize an operation of this scope 10,000 kilometers away! And this wasn't a guerrilla operation. We were directing a regular war. How could a small country, without the great resources of the Soviet Union or the United States, supply an operation at that distance? How could it defeat an army such as South Africa's, along with the Zairean army and the mercenaries?

Chui is a witness. He was in the command center where, night after night, Fidel directed operations.

Fidel knew the terrain in Angola better even than those of us who were over there. "Go to such-and-such river, at such-and-such hill," he'd say in his cables. It was just like the Sierra Maestra, which he knew like the back of his hand. "Go to the top of such-and-such hill," he'd say. He would send a message to Che, to Ramiro [Valdés]: "Take such-and-such position." In Angola it was the same. He'd send a message to General Leopoldo Cintra Frías, who headed the military mission during the final stage: "Polo, position three tanks on such-and-such road. Don't let yourselves be outflanked."

WATERS: Numerous ranking Cuban officers gave their lives in Angola. Chui mentioned Raúl Díaz Argüelles, his commander and head of the mission. Raúl [Castro], in one of his tributes to those who fell in combat in Angola, noted that a quarter of them were officers. Chui, you yourself were seriously wounded. How did that happen?

CHUI: It was while my combat brigade was being transferred to Malanje province in northern Angola. On March 5, 1988, I was riding at the head of the third convoy, the one in which the weaponry was being transported. My vehicle set off a reinforced antitank mine, and I was thrown almost twenty meters. I was in critical condition.

Our commander in chief sent a plane to take me back to Cuba, given the gravity of my state. After quite a battle, medical science was able to save my life. But they had to amputate my right leg, which was in very bad shape. Typical of Fidel, he would ask about my health every day and gave precise instructions on what actions to take. I was treated first in the Brothers Ameijeiras Hospital by a very competent multidisciplinary team. Later, for my recuperation, I was transferred to the Center for Surgical Medicine Research, and I finished my rehabilitation at Carlos J. Finlay Military Hospital.

Sío Wong: In our army the leader is an example. We believe this is very important. This is also true for the revolutionary cadre. It's part of our code of ethics for cadres. The leader has to set an example.

This was always a characteristic of Che, who was incapable of giving an order he himself was not prepared to carry out. And it's equally true of Raúl and Fidel.

During the revolutionary war, as I mentioned earlier, compañeros had to write to Fidel asking him not to participate in combat. The same went for Raúl in the Second Eastern Front. Because Fidel and Raúl frequently put themselves at risk in combat. That's one of the reasons people follow them. It's a quality that Raúl has inculcated in our military leaders. They're first in combat, first in setting a personal example of austerity in the way they live.

The imperialists and counterrevolutionaries, including the Miami mafia types, have created a harsh and even bloodthirsty image of Raúl, but the truth is totally the opposite. I've known Raúl for more than forty years, seven of them working directly with him. He's a man of deep human sensibility. His entire life has been dedicated to fighting for the people. He's capable of attending to the country's most important problems while being attuned to the family and personal matters of individual compañeros and to what ordinary people face.

In private life, away from service, we're friends. I get together with his family, and sometimes my sister Angelita invites him over for a Chinese dinner. But at work he's the minister and I'm his subordinate. He's very straight and demanding.

That's why we've been able to organize armed forces with that discipline, devotion, dedication, prepared for anything. As Fidel has said publicly, Raúl is the organizer of a disciplined army, a proletarian army.

CHOY: Raúl demands discipline—the same discipline he himself has. You see it in the way he dresses. Sometimes he demands that a person put his cap on, or button his shirt. But he himself follows the dress code of the armed forces strictly. His uniform is always buttoned correctly.

Cuba's strategic mission

WATERS: During the time the Cuban volunteers were in Angola, you had to contend with UNITA, the Angolan force headed by Jonas Savimbi, which had South African and U.S. backing.[27] What was the approach of the Cuban armed forces toward UNITA?

SÍO WONG: We didn't participate directly in Angola's struggle against the UNITA bandits led by Savimbi, who stood in the way of consolidating Angola's independence. We advised the Angolan armed forces, but we didn't participate in combat against UNITA.

We were there to help the Angolans, along with the Namibians, against South Africa's intervention, against aggression from the outside. Not to support any one of the groups within the country. It's important to state that clearly. We were very, very careful that our troops didn't directly participate in combat among Angolans.

Fidel has explained this numerous times. The strategic mis-

27. See glossary, UNITA.

sion of our troops was to repel an invasion from South Africa and prevent an invasion from Zaire. We went no further than the border with Namibia. Internal problems must be resolved by those involved, by the belligerents themselves. That's always been our clear stand.

CHOY: We fought UNITA only when UNITA attacked us. Our strategic mission was to prevent an invasion by South Africa or Zaire that would destroy the revolutionary, nationalist, independence process in Angola.

CHUI: Civil wars are very cruel. Citizens of the same nationality, even family members fighting against each other.

SÍO WONG: We also had to be very careful because, as Chui said, the Angolans had Soviet advisers as well as our own. It was very complex.

We had many arguments with Soviet military leaders concerning the structuring of the popular armed forces of Angola. Because their thinking and our thinking ran in two totally different directions. The Soviets were for creating large divisions, tank brigades, a classical army. But in our high command, Fidel insisted that the Angolans needed light units, not large units. That the forest wouldn't accommodate big tank units.

In case of foreign invasion, we were there with small tactical groups. They were composed of an infantry unit, a tank unit, artillery, antiaircraft defense, designed to move very rapidly, with great maneuverability.

Moreover, we knew through our intelligence that the South Africans had seven tactical nuclear weapons. We had to take that into account. The Americans knew this too but permitted the South Africans to have them. A nuclear weapon wipes out a large unit at one blow. We had to have small units that would not be as vulnerable.

CHUI: We had to take into account the length of supply

lines, too. Provisioning these smaller units wasn't as massive a job.

Sío Wong: So we had long arguments with the Soviets, and we never came to an agreement. But time proved us right.

Negotiations with South Africa

Koppel: Choy, when were you in Angola?

Choy: I served in Angola in 1980–81. I was deputy head of our Anti-Aircraft Defense and Air Force there. The commander in chief and the minister of the FAR also assigned me to work with my Angolan counterparts to organize Angola's antiaircraft defense and air force.

This wasn't an easy task, since it involved very close coordination with the Soviets. The Soviets sent the weapons and we sent the personnel.

Koppel: What did you do after returning from Angola?

Choy: When I got back to Cuba in 1981, I held various leadership posts in the Anti-Aircraft Defense and Revolutionary Air Force (DAAFAR).

In December 1986 the Council of State named me ambassador to Cape Verde, a position I held until 1992. During that time, on Sal Island, which is part of the Cape Verde Islands, the agreement with the South Africans was reached following their defeat in the battle of Cuito Cuanavale. The governmental accord was signed later at the United Nations in New York, but the basic agreement was achieved at Sal Island on July 27, 1988, between the South African, Angolan, and Cuban delegations. The essence of the agreement was that the South Africans would pull out of Angola for good, provided that Cuban armored units halted our advance before reaching the Namibian border and pulled back to a line north of the Cunene River, in southern Angola.

On the very day the Sal Island proposal was reached, the

vanguard of General Enrique Acevedo's tank brigade, which was the forward detachment, had crossed the Cunene River. Behind it were a number of other brigades. We were practically at the Namibian border. The South Africans were in shock at this turn of events. There's an anecdote from the Sal Island negotiations.

As I mentioned, the South Africans had stated their willingness to leave Angola for good if Cuban military units stopped our march toward the Namibian border and returned to a line north of the Cunene River. The South Africans set the line. When the Cuban military delegation studied that line, they realized it was very close to the river. When it rained the area turned into a swamp, and the tanks wouldn't be able to move from there, posing the real danger that hundreds of these armored vehicles could become sitting ducks in case the war resumed. So our delegation offered to set a line even farther away from the Namibian border.

When this offer was made, the South African response was: "The Cubans aren't so bad after all!"

There was a second meeting at Sal Island a year or so later to review the implementation of the agreement. The South African delegation at that second meeting was headed by first vice minister of foreign relations Van Heerden, who dealt with the Angola question for them, plus four of their generals. Our delegation included General Leopoldo Cintra Frías (Polito) and myself.

The South Africans first tried to bribe us. Van Heerden began by explaining that South Africa was devoting 500 million rand [US$200 million] annually to "sustaining" Namibia. He said they were ready to continue giving Namibia this money provided there was peace at the border. What did that mean? That there would be no support for the African National Congress (ANC) and other movements in South Africa. They were practically asking us to commit a betrayal, in other words, and to pressure SWAPO [South-West African People's Organisation of Namibia] to betray the antiapartheid struggle in South Africa. Of course, the political leadership of our country didn't agree.

At one point in the meeting, the head of our delegation, Carlos Aldana, turned to Gen. Cintra Frías and said, "General, please tell Mr. Van Heerden how much weaponry we've withdrawn."

Polito gave the number of men, artillery pieces, and tanks —800 of them.

Van Heerden's mouth dropped.

He knew that even after that withdrawal, thousands of artillery pieces, tanks, other motorized vehicles, and men still remained with our forces in southern Angola.

"And what are you going to do in Cuba with so many tanks and so much artillery?" Van Heerden asked.

"They'll probably go to the Territorial Troop Militia" was our response.[28]

His mouth was still open. Clearly the South Africans would have been unable to stand up to that force advancing toward the Namibian border.

All of Cuba behind Angola effort

WATERS: General Sío Wong, what were your duties?

Sío WONG: I served in Angola in 1976. I was logistics chief for the military mission—a mission 10,000 kilometers away carried out by a small country.

I remember reading an article in the *New York Times* reporting that the U.S. government was shocked at the operation we had carried out. It spoke about the extraordinary logistical support, saying Cuban soldiers in the trenches didn't lack

28. See glossary, Territorial Troop Militia.

even for Havana Club rum. That was a lie, of course. Maybe they were thinking about how U.S. soldiers get their holiday turkey, their ice cream, and so on.

Support, yes. The combatants need a certain minimum of logistical support. We were able to do that because we are a socialist country. Within the bounds of our material limitations, all the resources necessary were made available.

You've got to give credit to the courage of compañeros who boarded the old Britannias. By the mid-1970s, when the Angolan mission began, those obsolete four-motor prop planes were practically out of service. We installed some additional fuel tanks so they could reach Sal Island off the coast of West Africa. They first had to make a stop in Guyana, then on Sal Island. So the trip to Angola by the first instructors was done in three legs. To fly in those Britannias you had to be brave, willing to risk your life. Later the Soviets approved the use of IL-62 planes for a number of flights, to transport some of our troops. There were ten flights during the early stages of the mission, I recall. I was on one of them.

We transported thousands of troops and large amounts of combat matériel. It was a secret operation utilizing a number of ports. We used our merchant fleet for sea transport. This could only have been done by a country like Cuba, with that type of spirit of solidarity.

I repeat: for these internationalist missions, we put the entire country behind the effort. Because we felt it was for something vital.

No, we didn't send bottles of Havana Club, but we did assure the essentials. We maintained a 10,000-kilometer supply line. That's something done by powerful countries such as the United States and Russia, countries with vast air and naval fleets. The U.S. military, for instance, draws up contingency plans for its forces to wage wars on two fronts at the same time. They have the weaponry to do so. They have the supplies, the logistics.

As the one who headed logistics, I took a direct personal interest in the *New York Times* article I mentioned. But the effort was accomplished only because the entire country was mobilized behind it, with the goal of maintaining supplies for the troops. This chapter in our history has not yet been fully recorded, but it was a real feat.

From the human side, our troops went to Angola as part of an internationalist mission. That, too, was part of the anonymous work carried out by our people. They didn't ask where someone was being sent, nor could we tell them. A regiment would embark from the port of Nuevitas in Camagüey. So a story would circulate to the effect that the Havana regiment was going on maneuvers at the FAR's national live-fire range. The regiment would embark at night, in secret. It traveled without an escort. The vessel could easily have been sunk. Imagine a ship carrying a thousand soldiers that could easily have been attacked by a high-speed pirate vessel firing a bazooka blast. We were running a risk. That's why it had to be secret.

Someday the military academies will have to study this. How was it possible? Clearly it was the participation of the entire people.

CHUI: A base of support for this effort existed among the general population. That's without a doubt. The people could see the leadership vision that was being demonstrated. They had confidence in Fidel as a leader. Even though the battlefield was in Angola, they understood perfectly the instructions coming from here in Cuba. And they followed them.

A turning point in history of Africa

KOPPEL: In the United States people know very little about what the Cuban Revolution has done to aid anti-imperialist struggles in Angola and elsewhere in Africa. But there will be a lot of interest in learning about this.

CHUI: We were a decisive factor during the 1970s in winning the independence of the Portuguese Empire's three major colonies on that continent—Angola, Mozambique, and Guinea-Bissau and the Cape Verde Islands. Nevertheless, these facts aren't stressed very much.

In the case of Guinea-Bissau, for example, the PAIGC [African Party for the Independence of Guinea-Bissau and Cape Verde] led by Amilcar Cabral requested Cuban aid in fighting for the independence of their country. And our troops played an important part in the defeat of the Portuguese army, leading to the liberation of most of Guinea-Bissau by 1973. That event shook the Portuguese government, contributing to the "Revolution of the Carnations" in 1974. From this came a "domino effect" with the independence of the Portuguese colonies of Angola, Mozambique, and São Tomé and Príncipe.[29]

Choy knows this history well from the time he spent as ambassador in Cape Verde.

The case of Angola merits special attention. Our troops remained there fighting together with the Angolan people for more than fifteen years. Not only did we help defeat the South African army, but we also helped bring about the elimination of apartheid and the independence of Namibia.

From our efforts in Africa, the Cubans brought back nothing material for Cuba. Only our wounded and dead, and the satisfaction of a duty fulfilled.

Sío WONG: History demonstrated we were right. We were

29. The Portuguese dictatorship was toppled in April 1974 (see glossary, Portuguese revolution). Mozambique obtained its independence in June 1975. São Tomé and Príncipe became independent in July 1975; Angola in November 1975.

not fighting just for Angola. From a strategic point of view, we were fighting against apartheid. And indeed at Cuito Cuanavale, after we broke the back of the apartheid army, they had to come to the negotiating table, grant independence to Namibia, free Nelson Mandela, and accelerate the process that soon led to the destruction of the apartheid system itself.

Angola strengthened Cuban Revolution

WATERS: What was the impact on Cuba itself? Not everyone agreed with expending such resources, with staying the course for so many years. How did the anti-imperialist struggle in Africa strengthen the Cuban Revolution?

CHOY: Well, it really strengthened us from an ideological standpoint. All of us who went had studied slavery, the exploitation of man by man, the exploitation of the countries in southern Africa. We had studied the evils that colonialism had wrought and was still creating. But we'd merely read about it in books.

In my own case—and I'm sure the same thing happened to other Cubans—I got there and could see with my own eyes what the colonial system really was. A complete differentiation between the whites, the Europeans—in this case the Portuguese—and the native population. We saw how these countries were exploited. We saw a country that was so rich, yet Angolans were living in what we saw as subhuman conditions. Because their country's riches were being stolen. Because the colonialists had not preserved the forests or the land.

Sometimes we'd be traveling in vehicles, and people walking along the road would run when they heard us coming. We learned why. Under Portuguese rule, if the native inhabitants didn't get out of the way, the colonialists would sometimes run them over. This went on for generations. So whenever they heard a vehicle coming, they'd run. And not just off to the shoulder of the road either. They ran because they'd been mistreated like this for years, for centuries.

The main lesson I learned from this mission was to fully appreciate colonialism's cruelty toward the native population, and the naked theft of their natural resources. To see a country with great natural wealth like Angola, yet with a population facing needs of the most basic type!

That's why I say that knowing the truth strengthened us from an ideological standpoint. The same thing happens whenever we see how a layer of the population in capitalist countries lacks the most basic necessities. The first time I went to Madrid, for instance, it was December. It's cold there that time of year. In the Gran Vía, the main street of that large city, I saw people sleeping on the sidewalk near a heating vent, with bags and newspapers over them.

You read about things like that in books, and you believe they're true. But until you see them for yourself, you can't fully understand the reality Karl Marx wrote about. That, I believe, is one of the lessons we all learned from internationalist missions.

These are the same lessons our doctors have learned, our athletic trainers, and other specialists who go to many countries. This includes countries that have natural riches, yet suffer tremendous backwardness and have great contrasts. The resources aren't used to help the masses of the people. And such backwardness isn't only in Africa. It's in the Americas too.

Bolivia, for example, has many tin mines. It has oil and natural gas. Nonetheless, it's tremendously backward. Ecuador the same, even though it's one of the principal exporters of oil. There are permanent social problems, because much of the population lives in virtually subhuman conditions. Until you see these realities, you don't understand how deep the problem goes. You don't understand what the people need. Direct contact with these problems strengthens our understanding. Those missions made this understanding concrete.

On diplomatic missions, you see this same reality from a different angle. I was able to see the kind of pressure Washington and other imperialist powers bring to bear on these countries.

Once I was talking about something to Cape Verde's secretary of state for cooperation, the equivalent of a deputy foreign minister. He was a good person with whom we had good relations. "The U.S. ambassador spoke to me about this very problem," he told me, "and threatened that if our position was such and such, they would cut our economic aid." You read about things like this, but it's different when you hear them yourself. I had the chance to observe this when I was a diplomat. You can't speak out about these things publicly sometimes. I thought the Cape Verdeans should have made a statement, but they didn't. And these were friendly countries. But they avoided speaking publicly about something that would clash with U.S. interests.

That's how it was.

CHUI: As Choy was saying, this experience helped all of us develop politically and ideologically. But the biggest impact was among the soldiers. In Angola and other countries of Africa, they could fully grasp the illiteracy, the misery, the lack of education, the lack of sanitary conditions and health care—conditions that people continue to live under.

Let me tell you a story. One time we slaughtered a pig, and I told one of the Cuban soldiers to give a piece of the leg to the Angolans. The Angolans said no, they didn't want it. When we asked why, they said they wanted the viscera, the innards.

That's what the colonial masters always used to give them, and they had developed a taste for it. They really didn't like anything else. They weren't used to it.

Our internationalist combatants observed what people in these countries lack, things we don't lack in Cuba. They learned, in general, a whole series of lessons, and acquired valuable experiences about the inequalities and injustices of today's world.

There are many in the world who denigrate our stance of helping the peoples of other countries who are fighting imperialist oppression. But within Cuba it enabled us to consolidate the political and ideological development of the young people who went to fight and to assist other peoples, who understood the justice of their cause and were later proud of their mission. You couldn't find a better example of this than the Five Heroes being held prisoner by the empire because of the internationalist mission they were carrying out to defend the people of Cuba against terrorist attacks. They are part of this generation, and three of them served in Angola.[30]

30. In September 1998 the FBI announced ten arrests, saying with much fanfare that it had discovered a "Cuban spy network" in Florida. In June 2001, five defendants—Fernando González, René González, Antonio Guerrero, Gerardo Hernández, and Ramón Labañino—were each convicted of "conspiracy to act as an unregistered foreign agent." Guerrero, Hernández, and Labañino were also convicted of "conspiracy to commit espionage," and Hernández of "conspiracy to commit murder." Sentences were handed down ranging from 15 years, to double life terms plus 15 years. The five revolutionaries—each of whom has been named "Hero of the Republic of Cuba"—had accepted assignments to infiltrate counterrevolutionary groups in the United States and keep the Cuban government informed about terrorist attacks being planned against the Cuban people. Millions worldwide mobilized to condemn the convictions, sentences, and harsh conditions

Sío Wong: On top of the things the compañeros have described, you have to add what our young doctors experience when they go to other countries. It sickens them. They see patients die before their eyes because the person doesn't have money. That's something that doesn't happen in Cuba. Such life experience means more than a hundred classes from a manual on Marxism. It's tremendous training for young people.

Right now we don't have any internationalist combat missions. We have other kinds of missions—as doctors, teachers, and more. But the simple fact that compañeros go and live in a capitalist country has a profound impact. This is something the three of us lived through growing up. But it's not something our young people today have experienced.

You can say many things to your children about what the past was like. When I was young, I recall, my brothers and sisters would tell me about the Machado dictatorship in the 1930s. They'd tell me about the big economic crisis of those years. But it's not the same as when you see, feel, live it yourself. If someone says, "Capitalism is like this; capitalism is like that," it's not the same thing. No, go live it. This is an experience for all our young people, because those who go—doctors, teachers, technicians, specialists—convey it to their entire family.

---

of detainment and demand their release.

In August 2005 a federal appeals court in Atlanta reversed the convictions and sentences and ordered a new trial in a different location, ruling that "pervasive community prejudice against Fidel Castro and the Cuban government and its agents and the publicity surrounding the trial and other community events combined to create a situation where [the defendants] were unable to obtain a fair and impartial trial" in Miami-Dade County.

René González served as an internationalist volunteer combatant in Angola during the late 1970s. Fernando González and Gerardo Hernández served in the late 1980s.

WATERS: Did the internationalist mission in Angola have an impact on Cuba's defense preparedness?

SÍO WONG: I wanted to talk about that aspect too, about how useful this was for us. More than 300,000 Cubans got actual combat experience in Angola. That's something the Pentagon has to take into account when they make their analyses.

Certain things are now being declassified, such as some of the previously top secret documents from the October Crisis of 1962. They reveal quite concretely how U.S. leaders weigh their decisions. Kennedy asked the Pentagon chiefs how many casualties they would suffer in an invasion of Cuba, and they told him the estimate was 18,000 in the first ten days. The price would be very high. Very costly.[31]

During the October Crisis, as the commander in chief said, no one trembled or flinched. Our people are quite willing and ready, quite firm and determined.

That's what the Pentagon has to take into consideration.

---

31. This episode is described in *Making History*, pp. 64–65.

War of the entire people

WATERS: General Sío Wong, the assignment you've had for nearly twenty years—president of Cuba's National Institute of State Reserves—is closely tied to Cuba's defense. Can you explain what the reserves are?

SÍO WONG: The National Institute of State Reserves (INRE) was established in 1981. During the 1960s and 1970s the government had put aside reserves for wartime or other emergencies. And the FAR had its own reserves. By the end of the 1970s, however, we recognized the need to systematically increase these reserves and to create a body that would take charge of directing and overseeing them.

INRE's task is to accumulate material resources to guarantee the economy's normal development and functioning in peacetime, to prevent disasters or attenuate their consequences, and to strengthen the country's defense capacities.

WATERS: You said INRE was formed in 1981. U.S. threats against Cuba were escalating then because of Cuba's solidarity with the new workers and farmers governments in Grenada and Nicaragua.

SÍO WONG: Yes, INRE was formed right at the time U.S. policy toward those revolutions hardened. Reagan had just become president. The Soviets had already told us we weren't under a nuclear umbrella. Raúl has explained this publicly.[32]

That's when we changed our military doctrine. We adopted the policy of the war of the entire people. That is, we defend ourselves with our own forces and means, based on each man, and each woman too, having a weapon—a rifle, a mine, a rock, something to fight the enemy with.

Our first reserve is the Territorial Troop Militia, founded in 1980 but whose origins date back to the Revolutionary National Militia created in 1959. In addition, a large part of the population is organized in Production and Defense Brigades.

Many friends point out that we didn't sign the treaty against antipersonnel mines. López Cuba explained it very well in *Making History*. Antipersonnel mines are the weapons of the poor. We have neither rockets nor atomic weapons. We have to defend ourselves. Moreover, mines are a defensive weapon, purely defensive.[33]

WATERS: And the State Reserves are a weapon of defense as well?

SÍO WONG: One purpose of organizing the reserves is precisely to strengthen the country's capacity to defend itself. We hope we won't be forced to use them in wartime. The

32. In a 1993 interview with *El Sol de México*, Raúl Castro recounted how in 1981 he had met with top Soviet leaders, including Communist Party General Secretary Leonid Brezhnev, to discuss responding to escalating U.S. threats. The Soviet leadership explicitly told Castro that they were not willing to defend Cuba against U.S. attack. "We cannot fight in Cuba because you are 11,000 kilometers away from us," Castro reported Brezhnev telling him. "Do you think we're going to go all that way to stick our necks out for you?" The interview was also published in *Granma* in April 1993.

33. *Making History*, pp. 42–44.

best way to win a war is to prevent it. To prevent it we have to be strong.

If we were to mark a moment that demonstrated these defense preparations, it was the Bastión 2004 strategic exercise held in December of that year. The entire country participated. Hundreds of thousands mobilized on the final day of the exercise, which lasted almost a week. It had been nearly a decade since such an exercise had been organized in Cuba. I think the last one was in 1996. Bastión 2004 was led by the commander in chief as president of the Council of National Defense. It proved our people, our country, are prepared to confront any aggression.

We've studied the U.S. wars against Yugoslavia and Iraq, and our people's preparation was intensified in order to strengthen the country's defense capacities. U.S. doctrine is to use technology and military power—air and rocketry—to bring their adversary to its knees with the minimum number of casualties to U.S. forces. That's what they did in Yugoslavia. That's what they were trying to do in Iraq too. They thought they could make it a cakewalk.

During the war in Yugoslavia the U.S. armed forces used their air power to bring the Yugoslav government to its knees in seventy-nine days. If it had been possible to hold out another few weeks, world opinion would have continued shifting against the bombing. The Pentagon was analyzing what it would take to carry out an invasion. They knew a particular characteristic of Yugoslavia—that during World War II Tito's partisans fortified the mountains and in later years the country continued improving its defenses. We've sent military delegations there to study the Yugoslav defense system. All the necessary reserves are in underground tunnels in the mountains. So the seventy-nine days of U.S. bombings didn't affect even 1 percent of the Yugoslav military. NATO and the Pentagon came up with estimates as to the number of casualties they would sustain in the event of a land war. That's what they wanted to avoid. In the end, in any war you have to occupy territory on the ground.

Some callously referred to the U.S. assault as a television war. "Today we're going to bomb the thermoelectric plant, tomorrow this or that bridge," and so on. But with that they broke the political will of the Yugoslav government to resist.

That wouldn't happen in Cuba. Our people are not divided. And here our generals can't be bought, as happened in Iraq. Open a Swiss bank account and buy off the generals. The troops don't fight.

It's not that the imperialists can't bomb us, or invade us. In Vietnam the war lasted more than ten years. The U.S. had 58,000 of its troops killed. The resistance of the Vietnamese people made it possible to mobilize a powerful movement against the war within the United States itself. Eventually the U.S. rulers were forced to withdraw from Vietnam.

In case of an attack against Cuba, in just one year's time— that is, about a tenth of the time the Vietnam War lasted— the U.S. would suffer a minimum of 10,000 troops killed. That's the calculation we've made based on the preparation achieved by the Revolutionary Armed Forces and the people of Cuba, demonstrated by Bastión 2004. Among the people of the United States, opposition to the war would grow, as it did during Vietnam.

But to resist you must have reserves. To force the imperialists to decide whether they're going to fight on the ground and take the casualties that will affect support for the war— to do that, you must have reserves.

Our most important reserves are the patriotic reserves of our people. But we must also have material reserves. We are an island. We can be blockaded easily. That's what the U.S. government did during the "missile" crisis of October 1962.[34] Under such circumstances, what quantity of oil would be needed? What quantity of food to feed 11 million inhabitants? We can't depend on foreign oil, on the contingencies of the world market.

All countries have reserves. But the country that has the greatest assortment of items in its reserves is Cuba. Not just fuel, lubricants, food, medicines, and raw materials. But even paper and pencils, so schools can remain open.

There is a decree of the president of the Council of State in which Fidel defines our policy on the reserves. In the first "whereas" he says:

"The increase, preservation, and monitoring of the material reserves is an indispensable condition for the security of the nation, for feeding the population, and for the people's well-being."

That is the role of the reserves. That is what Fidel was explaining in January 2005 at the international economists conference when he talked about Cuba being militarily invulnerable and of working toward becoming economically invulnerable.

WATERS: Two broad economic and social challenges that are

34. In the face of escalating preparations by Washington for an invasion of Cuba in the spring and summer of 1962, the Cuban government signed a mutual defense agreement with the Soviet Union. In October 1962 U.S. president John Kennedy demanded removal of Soviet nuclear missiles installed in Cuba following the signing of that pact. Washington ordered a naval blockade of Cuba, stepped up its preparations to invade, and placed U.S. armed forces on nuclear alert. Cuban workers and farmers mobilized in the millions to defend the revolution. Following an exchange of communications between Washington and Moscow, on October 28 Soviet premier Nikita Khrushchev, without consulting the Cuban government, announced his decision to remove the missiles.

receiving considerable leadership attention are the problems in the electrical generating system and the effects of the unprecedented drought in several of Cuba's eastern provinces. These are strategic questions too, not unrelated to the reserves and Cuba's capacity to defend itself. Can you describe what you're dealing with?

SÍO WONG: Our national electrical grid was designed more than forty years ago. The system was the product of the favorable relations we had with the Soviet Union at the time. All the oil, the spare parts, the cables, the technology, everything, came from the Soviet Union. But to keep running, anything produced with Soviet technology had to have an oil tank attached. Plus a planeload of fuel for backup. Cars, trucks, tractors—everything was the same.

The entire electrical generation system is based on seven main thermoelectric plants that are interlinked. But that means the system is very vulnerable. If one plant fails it has serious repercussions for the whole system. Last year the turbine shaft of the Antonio Guiteras plant in Matanzas broke down. That is our most modern and efficient plant, built with French technology. We had to dismantle the shaft, contract for a plane, and send it to Mexico for repairs. With this plant's 350 megawatts offline, the whole system was destabilized.

Contributing to the electricity crisis has been a lengthening of the downtime for repair and maintenance. Since the beginning of the Special Period, we've increasingly used crude oil extracted here in Cuba to generate electricity. This has saved us millions. But this oil has a high sulfur content. It doesn't burn as cleanly, which means more downtime for maintenance.

The nuclear-powered generators we were building in Juraguá on Cienfuegos Bay were intended to complement this system, reducing its vulnerability. A second thermonuclear

"The Spanish crown brought in indentured Chinese labor as an alternative to African slaves. Between 1848 and 1874, 141,000 were sent from China to Cuba and a similar number to the U.S. In 1870 Cuba's population was 1.4 million; in the U.S. it was 38 million."

1. Contract, in Spanish and Chinese, for Chinese indentured laborers, 1861.

2. Chinese laborers building railroad in United States during 19th century. Thousands later emigrated from the U.S. to Cuba.

3. Black slaves cutting sugarcane in Cuba.

Biblioteca Nacional José Martí

Ismael Francisco González/Granma

1. Soldiers in Cuba's independence army, 1898.
2. Monument in Havana to the Chinese who fought in Cuba's independence wars. Inscribed on its base are the words of General Gonzalo de Quesada: "There was not a single Chinese-Cuban deserter. There was not a single Chinese-Cuban traitor."

"Thousands of Chinese participated in Cuba's war of independence. Of these, it is said, there was not a single deserter nor a single traitor."

Biblioteca Nacional José Martí

Library of Congress

1

"In Cuba before the revolution there was discrimination against blacks and Chinese. The Chinese population itself was class divided. There were both rich and poor."

In the late 19th and early 20th century, after bonded labor came to an end, Chinese communities developed in cities and towns all over Cuba. Most Chinese were engaged in petty commerce and trade. Some became very wealthy.

3

4

1. Reception for Chinese minister in Cuba, held in the Chinese Chamber of Commerce in Havana, 1940s. The painting in the background is of Chiang Kai-shek, Franklin Roosevelt, Winston Churchill, and Madame Chiang Kai-shek in Cairo, 1943. **2.** Chinese vendor in Havana, late 1940s or early 1950s.

3. Armando Choy (left), working in his father's store in Santa Clara, 1952–53.
4. During the 1940s and 1950s there were four Chinese-language dailies in Cuba. In photo, restaurant patrons reading *Man Sen Yat Po*, newspaper of Kuomintang Party in Cuba, 1949.

> ## "We were becoming increasingly conscious of the unjust character of the Batista regime. When the July 26 Movement was founded, we joined it."

Bohemia

Granma archives

1. On March 10, 1952, Fulgencio Batista toppled Cuba's elected government and established an increasingly brutal dictatorship backed by Washington. In photo, Batista with his troops on day of coup. **2.** Fidel Castro organized a revolutionary movement to overthrow the tyranny. Its opening act was an assault on the Moncada army garrison in Santiago de Cuba on July 26, 1953. In photo, Castro and other captured combatants being led to jail a week later.

3. Armando Choy (front row, left) in student protest against Batista dictatorship, Santa Clara, May 20, 1957. The demonstration was quickly broken up by police. Choy and others were arrested later that day. **4.** Student demonstration in Havana under attack by cops, November 1956. **5.** Gerardo Abreu (*Fontán*) and **6.** Ñico López, leaders of July 26 Movement Youth Brigades, were instrumental in recruiting Sío Wong to revolutionary movement.

"'Hey Fidel, even the Chinese are here!' That was how I was greeted when I got to the Sierra Maestra."

1

2

3

During the 1956–58 revolutionary war, thousands of young workers, peasants, and students joined the Rebel Army and July 26 Movement to fight the Batista dictatorship.

1. Moisés Sío Wong after battle of Placetas, December 24, 1958.

2. Gustavo Chui, left, with members of Rebel Army tank company outside Havana, shortly after revolution's victory.

3. Armando Choy (back row, second from right), with fellow Rebel Army combatants, near Fomento, late 1958.

4. Sergio González (*El Curita*), at right, a leader of July 26 Movement underground in Havana. Photo shows him at printshop where clandestine revolutionary newspaper was produced. In February 1958 Fidel Castro sent Sío Wong on mission to Havana to instruct González to leave for the Sierra. González insisted on staying and days later was killed by Batista's police.

5. Fidel Castro and victorious Rebel Army columns entering Santiago de Cuba, January 1, 1959. That night, Gustavo Chui was among those guarding the rally where Castro addressed tens of thousands.

Granma archives

Granma archives

古巴華僑教民主同盟

PATRIA Ó MUERTE
ALIANZA NUEVA DEMOCRACIA CHINA

1. Members of Chinese New Democracy Alliance, an organization of revolutionary Chinese-Cubans, at rally in support of nationalization of U.S. capitalist holdings, July 10, 1960. **2.** Mass meeting in Havana's Chinatown, October 2, 1960, in in honor of 11th anniversary of Chinese Revolution. One week later the José Wong Brigade of the Revolutionary National Militia—named after a communist revolutionary assassinated in 1930 by agents of the Machado dictatorship—took the lead in driving all remaining centers of drugs, gambling, and prostitution out of Chinatown. **3.** José Wong.

"What was the most important measure to eliminate discrimination against Chinese and blacks? The principal measure was the revolution itself."

The 1959 agrarian reform and 1961 literacy drive were two sweeping measures that reflected and accelerated the working-class trajectory of the revolution. **4.** Fidel Castro and María de la Cruz Sentmanat, 106-year-old former slave who learned to read and write during literacy drive. **5.** Beach in Havana that was formerly "whites-only" private preserve for the wealthy. One of the revolution's first measures in 1959 was to make all beaches public and open to all.

*"We put all of Cuba behind the Angola effort.
We felt it was something vital."*

Granma

Courtesy Armando Choy

Courtesy Moisés Sío Wong

Reinaldo/Juventud Rebelde

Pastor Batista Valdés/Granma

In November 1975 the government of newly independent Angola asked Cuba for help in defeating an invasion by apartheid South African regime. That mission involved nearly 400,000 Cuban volunteers over a period of sixteen years.

1. Raúl Díaz Argüelles, first head of Cuba's military mission in Angola, killed by a land mine in opening weeks of campaign. **2.** Armando Choy (center) in Angola, March 17, 1981. At right is Gen. Ramón Pardo Guerra. **3.** Moisés Sío Wong, second from left, leading an operation in northern Angola, 1976.

4. Rally of Che Guevara Internationalist Teachers Detachment on the way to Angola, 1983. **5.** Cuban internationalist, at right, teaching Angolan combatants to read and write.

"Cuito Cuanavale was a turning point in the history of the struggle for African liberation." NELSON MANDELA

Pastor Batista/Juventud Rebelde

Juvenal Balan/Juventud Rebelde

Courtesy Gustavo Chui

3

Courtesy Gustavo Chui

4

In 1987–88 South African troops again drove deep into Angola. They were halted at Cuito Cuanavale, with Cuban troops decisive in winning the battle. Cuban and Angolan forces launched a counteroffensive, pushing southward all the way to Angola's southern border. Cuba mobilized its resources behind the effort.

1. Cuban forces building road in Angola, 1988. **2.** Cuban tank column in southern Angola, 1988.

3. Gustavo Chui (front, center) reviewing Cuban tank brigade in Luanda, 1987. **4.** Chui's jeep destroyed by an antitank mine, March 5, 1988. Chui was critically wounded, losing a leg.

> *"We were not fighting just for Angola. Breaking the back of the apartheid army at Cuito Cuanavale opened the process that soon led to the destruction of the apartheid system itself."*

1. Following its defeat at Cuito Cuanavale, South Africa sued for peace. In photo, signing of peace accords at United Nations in New York, December 1988. At table, left to right: South African defense minister Magnus Malan and foreign minister Pik Botha; UN secretary-general Javier Pérez de Cuéllar; U.S. secretary of state George Schultz; Angolan foreign minister Alfonso Van Dunem and ambassador to U.S. Antonio dos Santos Franca; Cuban foreign minister Isidoro Malmierca and Gen. Abelardo Colomé.
2. Returning combatants of Cuban women's antiaircraft unit in Havana, May 1989.

Margrethe Siem/Militant

Mary-Alice Waters/Militant

3. Johannesburg rally greets Nelson Mandela following his February 1990 release from 27 years in prison.

4. Mandela and Castro in Matanzas, Cuba, July 26, 1991. "We in Africa are used to being victims of countries wanting to carve up our territory or subvert our sovereignty," Mandela said. "It is unparalleled in African history to have another people rise to our defense."

"Some day we may have to erect a monument to the Special Period." FIDEL CASTRO

With the fall of the regimes in the Soviet Union and Eastern Europe in 1989–91, Cuba abruptly lost 85 percent of its foreign trade. A devastating economic crisis ensued. In what is known in Cuba as the Special Period, millions of workers, farmers, and youth organized to confront the challenges. By 1996 the economic decline had been halted.

Courtesy Moisés Sío Wong

1. At the end of 1991 an urban agriculture program was launched, turning vacant lots in Cuba's cities, towns, and villages into productive vegetable gardens. In photo, Raúl Castro (center) at experimental *organopónico* in Havana, December 27, 1987. To right, in dress is Ana Luisa Pérez, agricultural engineer who pioneered this form of production. At extreme left, Carlos Lage; in plaid shirt, Estéban Lazo; front left, Vilma Espín.

2. Despite severe shortages, long-standing environmental and infrastructure challenges, such as the contamination of Havana Bay, were taken on during the Special Period.

Courtesy Armando Choy

3. Holguín, 1993. To ease the transportation crisis, millions of bicycles were imported from China, and more were produced in Cuba. **4.** Worker at bicycle factory organized by youth, Santa Clara, 1994. **5.** With fuel supplies scarce, animal traction was substituted for tractors, as on this Cienfuegos farm in 1994.

"Capitalism seeks to impose its culture, its ideas and values on all the peoples of the world. This is why the Battle of Ideas that our people are waging is of the utmost importance."

Some economic measures taken to confront the Special Period led to greater inequality, undermining social solidarity, the bedrock of the revolution. To address this threat, the Battle of Ideas was initiated in 1999. Spearheaded by the Union of Young Communists (UJC), it has grown to encompass more than 155 educational and cultural programs from primary to university level and beyond.

Angel González Baldrich/Granma

Juvenal Balán Neyra/Granma

1. Preuniversity class for workers at Camilo Cienfuegos sugar mill in Havana province, January 2003. Tens of thousands of workers and youth receive a regular wage as they study. University extensions have been opened in every municipality. **2.** To ensure that every rural school has access to television, videos, and computers, thousands of solar panels have been installed in the most isolated areas to provide electricity.

3. The Union of Young Communists mobilized youth to renovate schools and help build new ones throughout the country, making it possible to reduce class size and improve the quality of educational programs. **4.** Defense of the Cuban Revolution has always rested on the preparedness of its workers and farmers— men and women, young and old. In December 2004 some 4 million volunteers participated in nationwide military exercises, known as Bastión 2004.

> *"They call us subversives, and say we're subverting Latin America. But what can the imperialist system offer the peoples there?"*

DYN/Tony Gomez

Aizar Raldes/AFP/Getty Images

The capitalist depression that stalks Latin America has led to a rise in popular resistance across the continent, as workers and peasants respond to worsening conditions of life and work.

1. Working people in Buenos Aires, Argentina, in December 2001 protest government proposal to slash social spending, wages, and pensions in order to finance payments to imperialist bondholders on the country's $132 billion foreign debt. Days later government defaulted, plunging Argentina into deepest economic crisis since Great Depression. **2.** Workers march through La Paz, Bolivia, during April 2004 strike protesting rise of gasoline prices and demanding nationalization of Bolivia's oil and gas deposits.

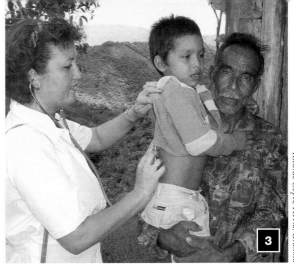

Venezuelan capitalists, backed by Washington, have sought to topple the government of Hugo Chávez and deal a damaging blow to working people there. In response to requests for help, since 1999 Cuba has sent thousands of volunteer doctors, dentists, technicians, and educators to Venezuela.

3. Cuban doctor treats Venezuelan child in rural area of state of Lara, July 2003. Some 15,000 volunteer Cuban doctors serve in Venezuela, living and working in neighborhoods where residents previously had little or no access to medical care. **4.** With help from Cuban volunteers, the Venezuelan government launched a mass literacy program spearheaded by youth. In photo, class in rural Carabobo state, July 2003. **5.** Organoponic vegetable cultivation in central Caracas, 2003. Program draws on experience of the last decade in Cuba.

> "We defend ourselves with our own forces and means, based on each Cuban having a weapon—a rifle, a mine, a rock. It's the war of the entire people."

March in Havana in front of U.S. Interests Section, March 2004. Sign saying "In Cuba this will *never* happen" depicts now-infamous photo of degrading U.S. treatment of prisoners in Abu Ghraib prison in Iraq.

plant was planned for Holguín. The nuclear plants were to augment and eventually replace much of the current system. This was the plan. But the Juraguá complex was a joint project with the Soviets, and in 1991 the Soviet Union fell.[35]

More than $1 billion had already been invested in the project. In order to complete it, another billion would have been necessary. Russia was not going to invest any more. We ourselves were not in a position to do so.

And there was another issue as well. Who were we going to depend on for nuclear fuel? Yeltsin? Putin?

We had no alternative. We decided to halt the work.

Fidel has outlined some of the steps we're taking to deal with the electricity crisis.[36] Cuba has doubled the amount of hard currency reserves to be invested in this area in 2005. Generators and equipment worth more than $280 million are currently being installed, which will give us a million more kilowatts of electricity within a year. The plan is to employ smaller and more efficient generators, spreading them more broadly throughout the country geographically and thereby preventing the loss of electricity due to transmission over long distances. Doing so will also protect against damages to the national electrical system and power cuts due to hurricanes, which hit us every year.

The increased electricity generated by this newly installed equipment will be supplemented by 500,000 kilowatts generated by a new plant just finished in the eastern region, and by

35. Work on the Juraguá thermonuclear plant was begun in 1983, with Soviet collaboration. Following the collapse of the Soviet Union in 1991, the project was mothballed. In 1997 Fidel Castro announced that there were no plans to revive work on the Juraguá reactor.

36. Castro's speech of July 26, 2005, in which he indicated some of these steps, was printed in English in *Granma International*, July 31, 2005.

increasing the number of generating plants online using natural gas that is a by-product of our crude oil production for fuel. Combined with measures to reduce energy consumption—like distributing new, more efficient pressure cookers and fans, repairing refrigerator door seals and thermostats, and exchanging incandescent light bulbs for energy-saving ones—these changes will effectively double the electricity available for production, services, and domestic consumption by the second half of 2006.

But that's the legacy we're dealing with today and why the problems are so great.

WATERS: And the drought?

SÍO WONG: This is the worst drought Cuba has ever recorded, hitting the provinces of Holguín, Las Tunas, and Camagüey above all. More than two and a half million people have been affected at the most critical times. We've had to distribute water by truck to two million people, and to animals as well. Camagüey is an area where there are large cattle ranches.

Despite the shortages of material resources, we've decided we have no choice. We have to go ahead with building two large water systems, plus the conduits to transport water to the affected areas. This is a gigantic undertaking. One of these projects in the central part of the island was started before the Special Period, but work on it was halted due to lack of resources, fuel, machinery, and so on. Now it's going forward again. It will carry water from the center of the country to Camagüey. The other project will begin in the eastern mountains where the most rain falls, in the Moa region. There we'll start building several dams. The system of conduits and canals and tunnels will carry water to Holguín, Las Tunas, and all the way to Camagüey.

These are enormous undertakings, and they will have a very great economic impact.

WATERS: The reserves have been important in confronting the intensified economic war against Cuba waged by the U.S. government the last decade and a half, haven't they?

SÍO WONG: Many compañeros don't realize how the U.S. government's economic blockade affects us.[37]

When I was young I lived near Havana's Malecón, the avenue along the seafront. I used to see the U.S. ferries that came and went every day, transporting merchandise. At that time our trade was overwhelmingly with the United States.

In recent years, we've spoken with U.S. congressmen from the South, and from other agricultural areas. In the National Assembly we received a delegation that included members of Congress from Louisiana. Before the triumph of the revolution, 36 percent of New Orleans's port trade was with Havana. You can imagine all the rice, corn, wheat, and oil we used to import from there. Now we import these items from places like Vietnam, China, and Malaysia. We even have to import powdered milk from New Zealand. We buy wheat in France. But the United States is just ninety miles away.

The blockade has cost us more than $80 billion in losses to our economy, just counting shipping and price differentials, and similar costs.

'A leader who has no reserves is a bad leader'

KOPPEL: When did you become president of the National Institute of State Reserves?

37. Washington has maintained an embargo on trade to Cuba since February 1962. With the 1992 Cuban Democracy Act (the "Torricelli law") and the 1996 Cuban Liberty and Democratic Solidarity Act (the "Helms-Burton law"), the embargo was significantly tightened in an attempt to deepen the economic crisis resulting from the collapse of trade relations with the former Soviet Union and Eastern Europe.

Sío WONG: I've carried that responsibility since 1986. But it's not the first time I've done something similar. During the revolutionary war, Fidel made me head of the Rebel Army's reserves for a time. Even then he called them the "strategic reserves."

"You're head of the reserves," he said. "Get to it."

We were keeping the strategic reserves in a little cave back then at the command post in La Plata. They consisted of ten 325-pound sacks of unrefined sugar, five cartons of condensed milk, and five boxes of canned sausages.

Some time later, Fidel came by after having toured the front for a week.

"So how's it going?" he asked. "How are the reserves?"

"There are six sacks left, commander."

"Six? How can that be? There were ten."

"Well, so-and-so came by. He didn't have anything to eat. And then what's-his-name arrived. And later someone else passed through with his platoon. They didn't have anything to eat, so I gave them a little sugar."

"Damn it," he exclaimed. "I put you in charge of the reserves, but you had no authority to give out a thing! Not even a spoonful of sugar."

He never said another word to me about the sugar. A few days later, however, Celia Sánchez brought me a handwritten note by Fidel. "Moisés," it said, "turn the reserves over to Otero. From now on you will concern yourself solely with the distribution of meat. Fidel."

I had been removed from my post and given a fictitious one; in those days we didn't have any meat to distribute!

I recalled this in 1986 when I was summoned to the offices of the Central Committee and informed that the Political Bureau had approved my nomination as president of the National Institute of State Reserves.

"Minister," I said to Raúl, "I was the first head of the strategic reserves, in the Sierra Maestra." I related the story of how I had headed up the reserves in the Sierra Maestra and been removed by Fidel. Then I said, "Tell the commander in chief that he may well be able to remove me for incompetence, for not doing my job well, for some mistake. But he won't be able to remove me for unauthorized use of the reserves." The commander in chief is the only one who authorizes their use. I'd learned my lesson.

When I returned to my office at the Ministry of the Revolutionary Armed Forces, I began to realize what those ten 325-pound sacks of sugar had represented. One gram of sugar has 4 calories. A glass of sugar water has 1,200 calories. With that you'll lose weight but you won't die. And with those reserves, the 200 men in the Sierra Maestra at the time could have gone for almost two months without getting anything from the outside. That's when I fully understood the importance of always having a reserve.

There's a saying that captures a deep truth: "A leader who has no reserves is not a good leader."

WATERS: How has the Special Period affected the reserves?[38]

SÍO WONG: During the period when most of our supplies came from the socialist camp, from the Soviet Union primarily—there was not much consciousness of the need for reserves.

When we set up INRE in 1981, we did a whole number of

38. In the first half of the 1990s, Cuba went through a deep economic crisis following the collapse of the regimes in the Soviet Union and Eastern Europe and the accompanying loss of 85 percent of Cuba's foreign trade. The political course adopted by the Cuban people in response to this crisis is known as the Special Period. For more on the Special Period, see part 3.

studies, with the help of the USSR. Different opinions existed on the role and place of this body, as well as who it should work under. Initially it was attached to the State Committee of Technical-Material Supplies (CEATM). At the end of 1985, given the inadequate attention being paid to development of the reserves, it was decided to separate off INRE from CEATM and to put it directly under the president of the Council of Ministers, Fidel.

I call that initial period the "lost decade." On the part of various bodies and officials there was a lack of consciousness about the importance of having reserves to confront any eventuality. Despite the instructions of the commander in chief and the calls of the minister of the FAR, it was necessary to wage a tremendous battle around this task. Before the Special Period there were many officials who argued: "If we don't have enough to eat, how can we put aside reserves?"

The Special Period showed that we had been wasting resources and that we could have accumulated a larger reserve. It also demonstrated the reserves' strategic importance.

The State Reserves enabled us to have fuel, to prevent the paralysis of basic economic functions like the sugar harvest, agriculture, and industry; food, to guarantee the basic ration; medicines, to save lives and prevent a single hospital from closing; even pencils and notebooks, to keep schools open.

We've advanced during the Special Period. But there's still a long way to go.

We don't use donations that come from all over the world as part of the reserve, although they're used by the government. The Cuban Institute for Friendship with the Peoples (ICAP) and the Ministry of Foreign Investment and Collaboration are responsible for keeping track of the receipt and distribution of donations.

A good example of why we have the reserves is Hurricane

Michelle, which struck Cuba in November 2001. We were able to repair all the hurricane damage, and we did it in less than a year. Because we could count on a reserve of fuel, food, construction materials, roofs, power poles and cables, and so on. We were able to deal with the damage to 160,000 homes in seven provinces, 13,000 of them totally destroyed.

In July 2005 Hurricane Dennis battered ten provinces, damaging more than 175,000 homes, among them 28,000 completely destroyed, with total losses reaching US$1.4 billion. It's the most destructive hurricane our country has faced since 1959. It was a Category 5 storm, the maximum on the Saffir-Simpson scale. The force of its winds reached more than 300 kilometers [185 miles] per hour. Some of the mountains in eastern Cuba suffered ecological damage that will take fifty years to heal.

In contrast to Cuba's approach, we've seen the consequences of natural disasters in countries far richer than we are, with much greater resources. A while back I was reading an article about relief claims made by people in Florida who had been affected by Hurricane Andrew, I believe. Andrew hit there in 1992—the "storm of the century," they call it—and people are still waiting for claims to be settled. They haven't received aid promised by the U.S. government more than a decade ago!

But within a year after Hurricane Michelle we had repaired everything. And since agriculture was also hit, we supplied an additional quantity of rice, grain, and oil to those provinces that were affected. That's the way we respond to any natural disaster. That's what we are doing now to deal with the damages inflicted by Dennis.

PART III

THE SPECIAL PERIOD
AND BEYOND

Courtesy Moisés Sío Wong

Responding to food shortages during the economic crisis of the 1990s, small-scale urban vegetable farms—*organopónicos*—were created in vacant lots in cities and towns across Cuba. This one in the Miramar district of Havana, described in the interview, was the first to become a productive and commercial success. Sign says "Buy here."

Facing the food crisis

WATERS: The development of small-scale farming, in urban areas especially, has been one of the important initiatives Cuba has taken during the Special Period. The creation of these *organopónicos*, as they're called, in every municipality was a response to severe food shortages Cuba faced in the early 1990s. It has led to marked improvements in quantity and quality of fresh vegetables available for most Cubans. Today the organoponics involve the labor of almost as many Cubans as does traditional large-scale agriculture.

General Sío Wong, you are one of the people who has helped lead this effort from the beginning, so you're in a good position to tell us about it.

SÍO WONG: Let me start further back.

When the revolution triumphed in 1959, more than 80 percent of the arable land was held by large private estates owned by Cuban and by U.S. ruling-class families like the Rockefellers, DuPonts, and Morgans, who had controlling interests in giant corporations such as United Fruit and the Cuban Electric Company. The U.S.-owned Cuban-Atlantic Sugar Company, for example, owned more than 600,000 acres. The United Fruit Company owned almost 300,000. There were cattle ranches of tens of thousands of acres in Camagüey.

During the early years of the revolution, the agrarian reform—carried out in two stages, the first in 1959, the second in 1963—established that there would be no landholdings greater than five caballerías. A caballería, one of the units of measurement we use here in Cuba, is 13.4 hectares, so that would come to some 67 hectares, or 165 acres. Everything above five caballerías—that is, the giant holdings of the U.S. ruling-class families and their corporations, as well as the big Cuban-owned plantations—was nationalized. Virtually all those landowners left the country, despite the fact they were offered compensation.[39]

As for the remaining land, the agrarian reform law turned it over to the peasants who had worked those parcels as sharecroppers, tenant farmers, squatters, or small sugarcane growers. Before the revolution these peasants mostly worked little plots of land, often paying rent in kind that could equal as much as half their produce. Nevertheless, the land didn't belong to them. So the revolution—their revolution—issued these peasants title to their land, up to 5 caballerías. A hundred thousand deeds were given out.

Through the agrarian reform, some 20 percent of the arable land became the holdings of small farmers, and 80 percent became state land. Our revolution had a policy of not dividing up the large estates, as occurred in other countries that had carried out agrarian reforms. That was a very wise decision Fidel and other leaders made, not to divide up the big holdings. State-owned sugar-producing enterprises and large cattle-raising enterprises were created on this 80 percent.

Early on we developed trade relations with the Soviet

---

39. Landowners were offered bonds that would mature in 20 years, at 4.5 percent interest amortized annually. The assessed value of their land was to be based on the value declared by the landowners themselves in October 1958 for tax purposes.

Union on favorable terms. When the price we had to pay the USSR for oil went up, so did the price at which we sold them sugar. On long-term contracts, which is how most sugar is sold on the world market, the Soviets would pay us up to 40 cents a pound, even if the market price had fallen to 10 or 15 cents. That was advantageous for us. The advantage for them was that producing beet sugar at home cost them up to 80 cents a pound.

We organized Cuba's whole agricultural production around those relations. We're often criticized for developing our agriculture that way. But it enabled us to build dams and reservoirs, bring electricity to the countryside, and create the whole agroindustrial infrastructure we now have.

By 1989, in fact, Cuba had more tractors per arable hectare of land than any other country in the world. Cuba has seven and a half million hectares of arable land, some 1.2 million acres, and in 1989 we had 110,000 tractors. There were so many tractors, and fuel was so cheap, that people didn't use them just for farming but even for transportation. To take a drive. To go visit your girlfriend.

From that point of view, economic relations with the Soviet Union were favorable for a small country like ours. The USSR benefited too from the standpoint of long-term stable supplies of sugar and, to a lesser extent, other products.

WATERS: From the very first days, as Fidel stated in 1960, self-sufficiency in food and diversification of agriculture was the goal of the revolution. But that's not what happened. Cuba's minister of sugar Ulises Rosales del Toro reminded the National Assembly of this a few years ago, noting that that strategy had been postponed because of the "market at fair and stable prices with the USSR and other socialist countries" you've been describing.

What did this concentration on sugar production and trade

mean for the cultivation of food crops?

Sío Wong: Cuba used to be an exporter of vegetables. There used to be a ferry from Havana to Key West. It took seven hours. My family lived by the Malecón, and I remember the steamship *Florida* coming in. I used to see trucks full of tomatoes, beans, and lettuce coming in to be loaded onto that ship.

But we came to be an importer of vegetables. In bottles and cans, the vegetables came from Bulgaria, Albania, the Soviet Union—in exchange for sugar.

Onset of Special Period

By the beginning of the 1990s, the Soviet Union and the socialist camp had fallen, and overnight the Special Period in Cuba began. The country was practically paralyzed. We had to adopt measures we had foreseen for times of war—in the event of a military blockade or aggression interrupting the flow of supplies. We referred to these measures, in their totality, as the "Special Period in Peacetime," since the same measures had been anticipated for a special period in wartime, facing the necessity to function without fuel imports and other resources.

We used to receive 13 million tons of oil annually, which we got from the Soviet Union on long-term trade agreements at special prices. It was bought with our sugar, as I described. Suddenly we had to begin working with 6 million tons of oil bought on the world market, at world market prices. Eighty-five percent of our trade had been with the Soviet Union and the other socialist countries. Suddenly, instead of being able to import $8 billion worth of goods, we had only $2 billion to buy a little oil, as well as essential food and medicines, on the world market. Our ability to purchase goods from abroad dropped by almost 80 percent.

All those gas-guzzling tractors stopped running. The buses

stopped running. The government of China began sending us millions of bicycles. Do you remember how Havana in the early 1990s started looking like Beijing, with millions of bicycles? Millions.

In 1993, in face of the economic crisis, the government took a whole series of measures in order to save the revolution. Many of them we didn't like, since they increased inequalities. We had always fought for a more just society, a socialist society, one that guarantees the basic needs of the whole population: health, education, food, housing, everything.

But we had no choice. One measure was allowing free circulation of the dollar. Previously it had been prohibited by law.[40] Agricultural markets were created, where farmers sold produce directly to the population at unregulated prices. Possibilities for self-employment were opened up. That's when the famous paladares arose—those little twelve-seat home restaurants, whose name *paladar* is taken from a Brazilian soap opera popular at the time. We began expanding inter-

40. With the collapse of production in the early 1990s the value of the peso plunged. Officially pegged at 1 Cuban peso to the U.S. dollar, by the summer of 1993 dollars traded for as much as 150 to 1 on the black market. In July 1993 circulation of the dollar was decriminalized, and stores were opened that sold imported goods for dollars. As the economic decline bottomed out during the Special Period and production recovered, the exchange rate stabilized at around 25 to 1.

As part of its stepped-up economic pressure on Cuba, Washington increasingly blocked Cuba's use of dollars in international transactions. In response, in November 2004 the Cuban government announced that U.S. dollars would no longer be allowed to circulate freely in Cuba. While Cubans are still able to receive U.S. dollars, both they and tourists must exchange dollars for what are known as convertible pesos (CUC), paying a 10 percent surcharge. Tourist hotels, restaurants, taxis, and "dollar stores" now accept only convertible pesos.

national tourism. And we opened up avenues for foreign investment, along with the creation of mixed enterprises.

We had to stop providing lots of things free of charge. We began charging for sporting events like baseball, for instance, although not very much. How much does it cost now? One peso, two pesos? Much less than in the United States, where a ticket to a baseball game can cost fifty or a hundred dollars.

We don't like the inequalities that have arisen between those who have dollars and those who don't. That's why the dollar stores were opened. They were established to bring in hard currency to pay for social programs that benefit everyone. Some of them even have the name TRD—Tiendas Recaudadoras de Divisas [Stores to Recover Hard Currency].

Creation of organoponic gardens

WATERS: What was the origin of urban small-scale vegetable farming?

SÍO WONG: I mentioned that one of the measures we took at the beginning of the Special Period was to expand tourism to bring in hard currency. But the expanding tourist hotels needed a growing supply of fresh vegetables. We had to fly these in from Mexico, Jamaica, and other countries. Our pilots began calling those trips "flights of shame." The tourism sector had to pay $35,000 for a single flight to bring in tomatoes and lettuce that, shamefully, were not being grown here.

On the wall here is a photo taken on December 27, 1987 [see photo section], a few years before the Special Period began. In it you can see Raúl Castro, Vilma Espín, and Carlos Lage visiting a military unit. During that visit Raúl encountered an engineer named Ana Luisa Pérez, who had planted vegetables in some plantain pre-germinators with good results. He gave an order to develop and generalize this form of cultivation. A directive to that effect was issued to military units. Out of this came what we now call the *organopónicos*. The name comes from the fact that most of the inputs are organic.

General Néstor López Cuba was the first to start organoponic cultivation. The unit was one hectare in size. That's 2.3 acres. At the time he headed the 50th division, located in eastern Cuba. The organoponic farm there was built next to the base where the unit was headquartered and was worked by the families of officers and soldiers. López Cuba was an old campesino. He liked doing this.

An armed forces center was set up in Havana known as Hortifar, mainly to produce vegetables.

So the organoponic gardens developed first within the armed forces. In the civilian sector we continued to import vegetables.

When the Fourth Party Congress was held in Santiago de Cuba in October 1991, the Special Period was just beginning. But it was already clear that our priority task was the food program. To produce food.

At the beginning of December, we held an assembly here at the National Institute of State Reserves and decided to create an organoponic garden. Fifty-four days later the first lettuce was harvested. We had already been clearing trash out of a vacant lot across the street, so we filled it with seed beds and planted. We started on December 5, 1991, and harvested the first lettuce on January 28, 1992—the anniversary of José Martí's birth.

Not everybody was happy with what we were doing, however.

I'll tell you a story. On December 31, 1991, at the military council within the Ministry of the Revolutionary Armed Forces, I informed the minister [Raúl Castro] that we had begun building the garden and that many people were criticizing us: "How is it that in the Special Period you're using concrete blocks and cement, wasting such scarce materials, to build an organoponic vegetable garden?"

Raúl answered them. "I know that some leaders are criticizing Sío Wong," he said. "But what they should do is follow his example and produce food. Moreover, I'm the godfather of that organoponic farm."

Then Raúl asked me, "Well, how much are you going to produce?"

I'd heard that in China they produce 25 kilograms [55 pounds] of vegetables per square meter per year. So I told him, "I think we can get 25 kilograms per square meter."

A compañero took out a calculator: 25 kilograms per square meter equals 75,000 quintals per caballería [7.5 million pounds per 33 acres].

"Seventy-five thousand quintals per caballería! Are you crazy?"

If you get 10,000 quintals per caballería a year that's a lot— 10,000 quintals of anything. Seventy-five thousand quintals would be extraordinary.

"Well," I said, "Let's try."

How did we start? First, we assigned two compañeros, the one in charge and the botanist. Then we created voluntary work brigades from the institute. For three years—1992, 1993, and 1994—we failed to go above 10 kilograms per square meter.

At the beginning of 1995 we requested permission to establish a new system of compensation, one that went against the established norms here in Cuba. Why did we do so? Farm work is one of the hardest jobs there is. This is true even of our conventional agriculture, which is mechanized with tractors, harvesters, and so on. Yet the average wage of a farmworker is 148 pesos. The average wage in Cuba is about 250 pesos.[41] So we requested permission to provide an incentive. It's more like a cooperative, where the land is owned by the state, like the UBPCs created out of the state farms in 1993. Let me explain how the system works.

A worker at the *organopónico* gets an advance of 225 pesos—similar to an advance on wages—to cover expenses. The workers are charged for all the inputs: electricity, water, seeds, etc. Then 50 percent of the unit's net profit is divided among the workers. That's the first principle.

The second principle: the shares aren't equal. Profits are distributed under the rule that those who work more earn more.

The third principle: the person in charge earns 10 percent more than the highest-paid worker, as an incentive to take on overall administrative responsibility. One of the chief merits of this system is that those who work the land—who have some of the hardest jobs—deserve to be paid in accordance with output.

In other countries—as we're now seeing in Venezuela—it's the middlemen who make the most. The producer, the peasant producer, gets paid the least. That's how it's done in all these underdeveloped countries. And the same thing was happening here, even though we have state-owned distribution and marketing enterprises.

At the end of 1995 I reported to the Military Council that we'd reached 30 kilograms per square meter. "So what's responsible for the miracle?" they asked.

There is no "miracle," I said. The results are due to systematic, sustained, intensive work. For 8 hours, 9 hours, 10 hours

41. These figures correspond to wages prior to 2005. In April 2005 the minimum wage in Cuba was demonstratively raised from 100 to 225 pesos a month. Over 1.6 million workers, including the overwhelming majority of farmworkers, benefited from this measure, which raised the average wage in Cuba to 312 pesos a month.

a day, out in the sun. Every day the plants have to be watered and tended. You have to come in on December 31, January 1, Christmas Day, May 1. There's no Saturday or Sunday off. Transplanting has to be done after 4:00 PM or else the sun will kill the plants. You have to weed, fertilize, thin the plants. You have to produce the organic material, everything.

But as a result, on that little piece of land you'll see 60 tons of vegetables produced per year. That's 30 kilograms per square meter of arable land, which comes to 300 tons per hectare. It's very intensive agriculture.

This is really when the movement to take advantage of all the free space in and around the cities began to take off.

We don't call it organic agriculture, because organic farming and organic products require international certification. There's an international agency that sets the standards. They come and measure the contamination levels and so on. But in fact we use virtually no chemical products. We use organic material and biological controls. That's why we say our farms are organoponic and agroecological. Our scientists work hard to find all the biological controls to fight pests. Because chemical pesticides, first of all, are very expensive and, secondly, can contaminate the environment. That's especially a concern here in the city. So we use organic materials and biological controls. We produce them in our laboratory here.

We use a localized irrigation system, invented by the Israelis, which is very efficient and uses a minimal amount of water. That too is an important strategic concern—to be able to grow food even if water supplies are disrupted, whether by drought or by enemy action. We also produce seeds for the entire country.

Growth of the movement

In 1995 there were only 257 hectares of organoponic agriculture in the whole country. To say it was OK for a worker to earn a thousand pesos a month was taboo. When Raúl Castro came here in 1997 after a trip we had taken to China, he looked out at the organoponic garden from my office on the fourth floor. It's not a crime to earn a thousand pesos a month through honest hard work—that was his conclusion. And he said so publicly.

After that, things began to change.

By 2003 we had 45,000 hectares of organoponic and intensive gardens. Look how production has increased. You can see it on the chart here. From 4,200 tons of vegetables in 1994 to almost 4 million in 2004.

We've now surpassed what I call conventional agriculture in output.

More than 380,000 people were working in small-scale urban agriculture at the end of 2004. About 420,000 work in conventional agriculture. Of the workers in urban agriculture, 82,000 are women. There are youth, mid-level technicians, almost 40,000 retirees, 10,000 professionals.

If you do the calculation, you'll see that up to twenty people can productively work each hectare. This chart shows how unemployment in Guantánamo was reduced from 7.1 percent in 2001 to 5.1 percent—in just two years. Santiago went from 9.1 percent to 2.9, Granma from 10.7 to 3.4. The greatest number of jobs created in recent years has been in agriculture—nearly 80,000 jobs. The overall unemployment rate by the end of 2003 was 2.3 percent. Internationally a rate less than 3 percent is considered very good.

The Special Period compelled us to develop this agriculture, although it was a tremendous battle. The United Nations Food and Agricultural Organization (FAO) now recognizes that Cuba is the one country that has been able to extend this small-scale agriculture on a mass scale. This is something the people of the world want: to develop an ecological and sustainable agriculture that provides the food the world's population needs, that protects the environment and reduces pollution.

We've been able to develop that in Cuba because Cuban workers and farmers made a socialist revolution. Agricultural production in Cuba is not driven by capitalist enterprises seeking to corner markets and maximize profits. It's driven by the need to provide abundant food for health and life.

Components of urban agriculture system

Those engaged in urban agriculture in Cuba are organized in several different ways. Agricultural production in Cuba is organized through several forms. All are engaged in urban agriculture.

There are state enterprises.

There are Agricultural Production Cooperatives, the CPAs, made up of farmers who have pooled their land. They own and work it jointly.

There are Credit and Service Cooperatives, the CCSs, in which farmers own and work their own land but help each other and share services and equipment, receiving loans from the government. They elect a directing board for the cooperative.

There are the UBPCs mentioned earlier, Basic Units of Cooperative Production. These were established in 1993 as former state farms were restructured and transformed into co-ops. The land belongs to the state, but the product of labor on the UBPCs belongs to the members of the cooperative who work the land.

Then there are the backyards. People farm in their backyards too.

And finally there are the "parceleros": anyone who wants a parcel of land to work can get one.

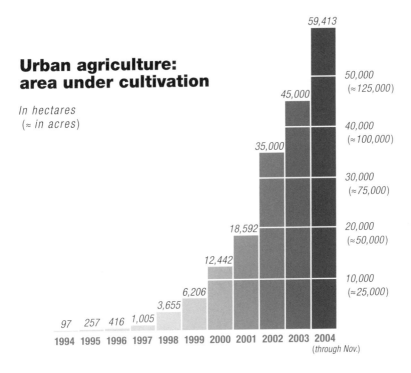

Urban agriculture:
area under cultivation

In hectares
(≈ in acres)

59,413

50,000
(≈125,000)

45,000

40,000
(≈100,000)

35,000

30,000
(≈75,000)

18,592

20,000
(≈50,000)

12,442

10,000
(≈25,000)

6,206

3,655

97 257 416 1,005

1994 1995 1996 1997 1998 1999 2000 2001 2002 2003 2004
(through Nov.)

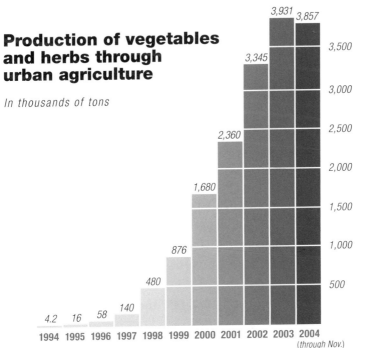

Production of vegetables
and herbs through
urban agriculture

In thousands of tons

3,931 3,857

3,500

3,345

3,000

2,360

2,500

2,000

1,680

1,500

1,000

876

500

480

140

4.2 16 58

1994 1995 1996 1997 1998 1999 2000 2001 2002 2003 2004
(through Nov.)

All these, to one degree or another, are engaged in urban agriculture, which is simply small-scale agriculture, nothing more. That's how it's known throughout the world.

We couldn't call it that at the beginning. Because our policy, in the Ministry of Agriculture and the leadership as a whole, was to develop large-scale agriculture, big enterprises. Small-scale agriculture was taboo. So we found another name: we called it urban agriculture.

But what is urban agriculture? Everything cultivated in the city of Havana and its surrounding area falls under that category. Everything within a ten-kilometer radius of the provincial capitals is designated urban agriculture. Everything within five kilometers of a municipality. Within two kilometers of each community with more than a thousand residents. That's all classified as urban agriculture. But it's nothing more that small-scale agriculture. The same thing is done in the city and its surroundings as in a small village.

That's how small-scale agriculture was developed throughout the country. It's both urban and rural.

This agriculture doesn't just have the potential to increase the quantity of food available for consumption. The United Nations Food and Agricultural Organization (FAO) recommends that adults consume between 300 and 400 grams of vegetables per day, no less than 300. It's what they recommend to get the vitamins and minerals the human body needs.

This is important, because the traditional Cuban diet consists of rice, beans, tubers, meat. Cubans ate very few vegetables. Maybe at Christmastime we ate tomatoes, lettuce, and radishes. But a culture of eating vegetables doesn't exist here. It's not like some other countries, like China, where it's a habit.

So in 2001—it was part of the Battle of Ideas and the improvement of education—Fidel issued instructions that child-care centers and schools would get food provisions through the urban agriculture system. This began here in Havana. Each organoponic garden, intensive orchard, or cooperative is linked to one or another school and also supplies child-care centers, old-age homes, hospitals, and so forth.

At our organoponic, INRE 1, for example, this practice had already begun in 1992. We provided vegetables to the day-care center on the other side of Fifth Avenue a few blocks away. Now the enterprise supplies produce to three child-care centers, plus the Cesáreo Fernández Elementary School, which we're godparents to and which we'll visit later today. Some 400 children eat lunch there each day, with a daily per capita of 125 grams of vegetables.

And we're making progress. Eating habits are beginning to change.

Take spinach. We began planting spinach. People didn't used to eat it. They called it Popeye food. Spinach has a lot of iron. Doctors began prescribing it for underweight children. So consumption is growing. People have gotten used to eating spinach, and now they ask for it. During the winter spinach grows a little slower, so that creates a problem.

The same with Swiss chard. People ask for it now. They eat it.

WATERS: How is distribution of food cultivated in the organoponic units organized?

SÍO WONG: It's sold directly to the population. The first principle: you sell it right where you produce it.

WATERS: There's no other distribution?

SÍO WONG: Yes, the Metropolitan Horticultural Enterprise, for example, has a warehouse. It buys produce and distributes it through state-run markets, sells it to hotels, to the tourist sector. It's a big enterprise with contracts with the farmers and also has its own *organopónicos*.

We have what's called free agricultural markets, which are based on supply and demand.

But there are others, where prices are regulated. Like our prices are regulated here. Prices can't go above a maximum that's been set. These markets are called *topados*—meaning the prices have ceilings.

WATERS: Are the topados state-run?

Sío WONG: Yes, a commission in the municipality meets monthly and fixes the prices. In the winter, for example, the price of lettuce goes down since production is high, but in the summer the price goes up. Each month there's a price list. There are some seventy capped markets here in Havana. Much of the production comes from the urban organoponic farms. And the Youth Army of Labor produces for the capped markets as well,[42] although their farms are in the countryside not the city.

The place where prices are totally uncontrolled are the farmers' markets, which I mentioned earlier. That is another type of market.

WATERS: Why would farmers sell in markets with price ceilings? Can't they earn more by selling in the unregulated markets? What's the incentive?

Sío WONG: Many farmers benefit from the regulated markets because they don't have a way to transport their produce for sale at the unregulated markets. They have to pay a middleman. So they sign agreements to sell to the topados. The consumer benefits as well, since the prices are cheaper.

42. See glossary, Youth Army of Labor.

Capitalism, socialism, and the environment

WATERS: General Choy, you are currently president of the State Working Group to clean up Havana Bay. The Cuban government decided to take on this massive environmental challenge during the Special Period. Like the response to the food crisis that Sío Wong has described, it captures some of the ways in which the revolution has been strengthened. As Fidel put it, "someday we may have to erect a monument to the Special Period."

How did Havana Bay get into such bad shape, and how did the project to clean it up come about?

CHOY: Havana Bay and its port bear the main weight in Cuba's import and export trade. That's been true since colonial days. Some 70 percent of all imports enter by way of the port of Havana. And excluding sugar and nickel, 90 percent of the exports. The Ministry of the Sugar Industry has its own ports, and nickel is shipped from Moa.

Prior to the revolution, as you would expect, the coastal ecosystem of the bay was not protected from indiscriminate contamination. During the early years of the revolution, the problem was recognized, but measures to clean up and preserve the bay weren't followed through.

It's not just the bay. The problem is also the hydrographic, or tributary, basin, which covers some seventy square kilometers. There are now 104 enterprises located in that zone that contaminate the bay.

Not to mention the sewer system, which is inadequate. Construction on the sewer system began in 1913 and finished in 1915. The city of Havana then had 300,000 inhabitants. The system was built for double that amount, for 600,000 people. But it now has to serve more than 800,000. There's insufficient drainage for all that water. So there's overflow in the streets.

Following the triumph of the revolution in 1959, various directives were issued and a few things were done. But there was no substantive progress. Commissions on the environment existed on the Havana provincial and municipal levels before the 1990s, and there were commissions on science, technology, and the environment in certain other areas—and still are. But an institution charged concretely with cleaning up the bay was not set up.

In 1996, 1997, and early 1998, as we were coming out of the worst years of the Special Period, the contamination problem was studied by Cuban research, scientific, and social institutions, with United Nations financing. The sources of the bay's dreadful environmental condition were determined. On June 15, 1998, the Executive Committee of the Council of Ministers voted to create the State Working Group for the Cleanup, Preservation, and Development of Havana Bay and its tributary basin. It's known by the initials GTE-BH (Grupo de Trabajo Estatal para el Saneamiento, Conservación y Desarrollo de la Bahía de La Habana).

The State Working Group leadership agreed to adopt the studies that had been done, as well as the twenty-one overall recommendations these studies had come to for cleaning up the bay. These recommendations became the basis of the group's work projections.

The first cleanup program was laid out over ten years, divided into two five-year periods. The year 2004 marked the completion of the first stage. The results are encouraging. Laboratory samples and tests of the water quality show a decrease in pollutants, and at the same time, the oxygen level has risen. This has enabled fish to begin returning to the bay, and following them, pelicans and gulls that feed on the fish.

Despite these small achievements, the waters continue to be in poor condition.

Intensive environmental and sanitation efforts are under way in collaboration with a number of national and international institutions, as well as some foreign governments, among them Belgium, Italy, Germany, and Japan.

Together with the Provincial Agricultural Delegation, reforestation of the bay's tributary basin has begun. Following the plan's completion in 2007, we will have planted more than a million saplings in order to purify and improve the capital's air quality and prevent the fertile land from being washed away with the runoff whenever there's heavy rain.

Together with the Provincial Directorate of Community Services, we are establishing a system to selectively recycle garbage first in the port area, and later throughout the entire basin.

Together with the Ministry of Public Health we're installing in the bay's outlet a system of seven atmospheric monitoring stations—the first of their kind in Latin America—that will automatically detect any negative variation in air quality and its origin. This will enable medical inspectors to locate the source of atmospheric contamination and demand that it be stopped.

We're building a large water treatment plant on the banks of the Luyanó River, one of the worst sources of contamination of the bay. It should be finished by the middle of 2006. This plant will be able to treat and purify up to 1,000 liters a second. In early 2005 construction began on another plant along the banks of the Luyanó. Its waters are very polluted because the river runs through San Miguel del Padrón, which has a larger number of factories than any other municipality in Cuba, and all the industrial waste goes into the Luyanó. Moreover, many people live along its banks, and the sewage water goes into the river.

The government's policy is to increasingly monitor the work done along the banks of the Luyanó, shifting production or moving enterprises that pollute the bay. For example, there were four slaughterhouses—three beef and one pork—that were relocated, because organic contamination from them was ending up in the river.

Related to the problem of the sewers, we received aid from the Japanese government to prepare a plan for draining rainwater runoff into Havana Bay and its tributary basin. Now we need to find the money to begin implementing the program in 2008. The plans call for the project to be completed in 2020.

KOPPEL: Does the Working Group have the power to enforce its decisions?

CHOY: Yes. We have jurisdiction over all questions concerning Havana Bay and its tributary basin. And we set demanding standards for everyone, including government ministries.

Last week, for example, I sent a letter to the minister of basic industry. There had been a big spill at the Ñico López oil refinery, contaminating the bay and adversely affecting the state of the water. The minister of industry, who I sent the letter to, is a member of the Political Bureau. But we have a mandate from the government and we carry it out. No provincial or municipal commission has authority to do what we do.

In addition, if anyone plans to remodel any factory located

on the bay or its tributary basin, or to build a new one, they have to submit the plans to us for approval. We analyze these projections, and then we inform the Ministry of Science, Technology, and the Environment (CITMA) whether we're in agreement. If we are, then CITMA gives the OK. If we don't give the go-ahead, they don't either.

This is a very complex effort. The entities contaminating the bay are responsible to eleven different ministries. These enterprises are spread out over ten of the fifteen municipalities in the capital. Each municipality has a vice president responsible for the environment, as well as a municipal environmental commission. In addition, there is a provincial environmental commission. In the area encompassing the bay and its tributary basin, there are forty-two people's councils. These are leadership bodies on the grassroots level.[43]

So we have to involve many people and many organizations in the work. It's a challenge, but we're achieving it.

And our example is being followed. In Cienfuegos the provincial government recently proposed that a similar project be undertaken there to clean up Cienfuegos Bay. Santiago de Cuba is also considering doing the same.

43. People's councils (*consejos populares*) were formed in neighborhoods, towns, villages, and rural areas of Cuba in 1992. They are local organs of People's Power, as Cuba's elected government bodies are called. The councils are composed in their majority, of elected delegates, plus representatives designated by the mass organizations (trade unions, women's federation, etc.), the Communist Party and Union of Young Communists, and the principal institutions and enterprises in the area. The councils are charged with maximizing efficiency in production and services in their area, and promoting the greatest possible participation and local initiative by the population to solve problems. They facilitate cooperation between the existing entities in their area, and monitor programs they develop.

Port of Havana

WATERS: You have another responsibility that's closely related, involving the operation of the Port of Havana.

CHOY: I'm the representative of the minister of transportation in the port of Havana, where I organize the port's administration. This is something new in Cuba.

A law on ports used to exist here. With various modifications, it went back to colonial days. In 2002 a new law on ports was adopted. It established a system of port administration, starting here in Havana. At that point I was named president of the administration of the Port of Havana. Like the State Working Group, it's something that never before existed in Cuba. We had to acquire experience as we went along.

Our work involves maritime operations at the port. We organize the arrival of ships, decide where they're going to dock, and supervise unloading, release of cargo, and shipping out.

WATERS: The port workers historically have been one of the most class-conscious and combative sectors of the working class in Cuba ...

CHOY: Yes, very combative, very revolutionary.

WATERS: ... and a large percentage of the port workers have always been black.

CHOY: Yes. In fact, in the ports, stevedores in Cuba were long referred to simply as the "blacks down below."

Today stevedores earn a very good wage, in addition to a bonus in convertible currency. Sometimes, depending on the number of ships that come in, they earn 50 or 60 dollars a month, up to 100 dollars. That's on top of their normal monthly wage, which is between 220 and 350 pesos. The administrators and those who work in an office earn less. The stevedores earn the most—the ones down below, carrying sacks, unloading ships, loading trucks.

The port works 24 hours a day. The work shifts are 7 hours, 20 minutes. In exceptional cases, the stevedores may agree to work twelve-hour shifts, but those cases are rare.

In addition, special attention is given to meeting workers' needs on the job, a job that is difficult and strenuous. It's extremely hot, for example, down below, in the ship's storage holds where the stevedores work. So, cold water is constantly lowered down to them.

KOPPEL: What you're describing reflects a different social reality from that lived by workers under capitalism.

CHOY: That's the point I'm trying to make.

WATERS: Let's go back to the fact that the clean up of Havana Bay was undertaken as an urgent task right in the midst of the Special Period. That's striking.

CHOY: In the early 1990s, when Fidel publicly explained the measures we'd have to adopt in order for the revolution to survive, he said at the same time: "We're not only going to conquer the Special Period, we're going to continue developing." The creation of the State Working Group for the Cleanup, Preservation, and Development of Havana Bay is simply living proof that as we have conquered we've continued to develop.

WATERS: Throughout the capitalist world, especially in countries under the thumb of imperialist domination, environmental destruction is accelerating. Whenever it's a question of cleaning up or protecting the environment, capitalists argue it costs too much. Why is this different in Cuba?

CHOY: In 1992, at the Earth Summit in Rio de Janeiro, Brazil, our commander in chief, Fidel, stressed the urgent need for taking measures to restore and protect the environment and thereby save humanity.[44]

Shortly after that, Cuba's National Assembly amended and broadened Article 27 of our constitution to spell out more explicitly the responsibilities of the Cuban state and people in relation to the restoration, preservation, and protection of the environment, and with it, of human civilization. We were the first country to do that after that summit.[45]

This is possible because our system is socialist in character and commitment, and because the revolution's top leadership acts in the interests of the majority of humanity inhabiting planet earth—not on behalf of narrow individual interests, or even simply Cuba's national interests.

44. In his remarks to the Earth Summit on June 12, 1992, Castro had pointed to the developed capitalist societies as "the main ones responsible for the appalling destruction of the environment.... It is not possible to blame this on the countries of the Third World, formerly colonies and now nations exploited and plundered by an unjust world economic order. The solution cannot be to prevent the development of those who need it the most.... Unequal trade, protectionism, and the foreign debt constitute ecological assaults and promote destruction of the environment. To save humanity from this self-destruction, there must be a better distribution of the planet's available wealth and technology."

45. The new Article 27 of the Cuban constitution reads: "The State protects the environment and the country's natural resources. It recognizes their close connection with sustainable economic and social development to make human life more rational and assure the survival, well-being, and safety of current and future generations. The competent bodies will carry out this policy. It is the duty of citizens to help protect the water, the atmosphere, conserve the soil, vegetation, and all the rich potential of nature."

The previous version of this article stated, "To assure the well-being of the citizens, the state and society protect nature. It is the responsibility of the competent bodies and also of each citizen to ensure that the waters and air are kept clean, and that the soil, vegetation, and animals are protected."

Cuba, Venezuela, and Latin America

WATERS: Sío Wong, you've spent a great deal of time recently in Venezuela, responding to a request to help develop the urban agriculture program there. Tens of thousands of Cubans are in Venezuela offering their services as doctors, nurses, technicians, teachers, sports instructors, and in other fields. How did this come about?

Sío WONG: What's developing in Venezuela is a revolution, in my opinion, a Bolivarian revolution. The banners of liberty and Latin American integration, first unfurled by Simón Bolívar, are being raised by a people who are showing themselves capable of confronting imperialism, neoliberalism, and the national oligarchy. Hugo Chávez Frías, the president, is a leader who is charismatic, honest, patriotic, and Bolivarian.

Venezuela is an immensely rich country, with untapped wealth. Not just oil. It's a country of a million square kilometers with immense land, water, and mineral resources. Fishing resources, water resources, lumber resources, mineral resources—including iron, bauxite, gold, and diamonds.

Yet Venezuela is a country in which 80 percent of the population lives in poverty, many in extreme poverty. You just have to go to the *cerros* of Caracas to see how 80 percent of the population lives. And this is in a country that's among the top five oil exporters in the world. It's the third-largest supplier of oil to the United States. It's a country that has the capacity to produce 3 million barrels a day.

It's estimated that more than $700 billion in profits was generated by workers in the oil industry there between 1958 and 1998. Yet more than two million people were illiterate. Many had no access to medical care or education. What did all the supposedly democratic governments do in the forty years following the overthrow in 1958 of the Pérez Jiménez dictatorship? That $700 billion was stolen from the Venezuelan people. That's what those governments oversaw.

So the current government came in proposing what Chávez called a social revolution. The emphasis is on social projects. For close to three years, the Chávez government was unable to carry out that perspective because the heart of Venezuela's economy is in the hands of the oil company, PDVSA [Petróleos de Venezuela, S.A.]. It's supposedly state-owned, yet the government did not have the resources available to move these social programs forward.[46]

This is not like the Cuban Revolution. The oligarchs and the rich didn't leave Venezuela because Chávez was elected. In the first couple of years after the Cuban Revolution triumphed in 1959, the workers and farmers carried out the agrarian reform, nationalized industry, and instituted other social measures. As that happened, all the rich, all the owners of plantations and companies, all the owners of mansions abandoned the country and went to Miami. That hasn't happened in Venezuela. They're still there. A large part of the economic power—the companies, the factories,

46. The government of Venezuela nationalized oil in 1975. When the businesses owned by foreign companies and Venezuelan capitalists became state property, however, the operations of the new company—PDVSA—were left in the hands of the previous management.

the markets, the stores, transportation—all these remain in private hands. The wealthy have the power of the media in their hands. For these reasons, it's a very different situation.

First the imperialist-backed forces carried out a coup d'état that was beaten back. Then there was the oil coup, and most recently the recall referendum.[47] After defeating the attempted coups and winning the recall referendum by a landslide, the Bolivarian revolution, the popular forces, are stronger politically and economically.

PDVSA is now the source of the financial resources and infrastructure to push forward social and economic programs, for example. Economic and political relations with countries of the Americas and the rest of the world have been broadened and consolidated. This has made Venezuela an important actor on the world stage, not just an exporter of oil. The

47. In an April 2002 attempted coup, Chávez and a number of his ministers and government officials were arrested. In response, hundreds of thousands of working people poured out of the poor neighborhoods of Caracas. In face of this massive show of support for the Chávez government, the military divided and the coup collapsed after two days.

In December 2002 the U.S.-backed capitalist forces opposed to Chávez began a "general strike," attempting to bring down the government. In reality this was a bosses' lockout, spearheaded by management at the state-owned oil company, and it initially paralyzed much of Venezuela's economy. Working people mobilized to restore production. Within two months the lockout, with dwindling popular approval, was defeated. The majority of the former executives of PDVSA were fired for their role in organizing the action.

In 2004 the imperialist-backed opposition tried once again to oust Chávez, this time through a recall referendum that took place August 15. With a massive, organized effort by workers and farmers throughout the country, the referendum was defeated, with more than 59 percent voting "no."

main thing is the leadership it is providing on the difficult road toward Latin American and Caribbean integration, fulfilling the dreams of Bolívar and Martí.

The Bolivarian Alternative for the Americas (ALBA), launched by Chávez and Fidel in December 2004 in Havana, marks an important step in confronting U.S. moves to exert greater hegemony through the establishment of the Free Trade Area of the Americas (FTAA).

Cuba's collaboration

KOPPEL: When did Cuban internationalist aid begin?

SÍO WONG: Chávez received our support and collaboration from the time of his victory in the 1998 elections onward. But it wasn't until the December 1999 disaster in Vargas that Cuba, responding to requests for help, sent a medical brigade, composed of hundreds of doctors.[48] Working under very difficult conditions, this brigade brought solidarity and aid to the victims and to the population as a whole. The medical brigades did a magnificent job. Afterward we kept up the collaboration, in these fields and others, through signed agreements between the two countries.

One of the first programs was Barrio Adentro [Into the Barrio]. It began in 2003 in the hills surrounding Caracas and was later extended to the whole country. It's a project of medical collaboration, with Cuban doctors working in the poorest areas.

At the same time, President Chávez asked for collaboration in developing a literacy program. We've had experience in that field in Cuba. In 1961 we mobilized a hundred thou-

---

48. In December 1999 mudslides and flash floods battered Venezuela's Caribbean coast, leaving up to 50,000 people dead. The state of Vargas was the hardest hit.

sand young people and taught more than a million people to read and write, eradicating illiteracy in a single year. Later we developed materials for literacy programs in Portuguese, English, French, and even Creole. We've had experience with programs in Haiti, in Africa, in many other places. So the Venezuelans asked for our help.

Our educators came up with a program utilizing videos that has revolutionized the speed at which students of all ages can learn. In Cuba the student-teachers lived with families for a year, including in the most isolated rural areas, and taught them using pencils, workbooks, and primers—the classic learning method. In Venezuela it's been possible to teach adults to read and write in seven weeks, with 64 half-hour lessons on video. This was done first in an experiment involving nearly 400 people, to see what the problems were. The results were that 87 percent of the students learned to read and write in seven weeks.

This program was extended to the mass level and named Mission Robinson.[49] Thousands of Venezuelan youth participated. The armed forces participated, providing needed logistical support to create fifty thousand classrooms throughout the country—each with a VCR, a television set, course materials, and facilitators.

It was the Venezuelans themselves who did this. It's said that we sent thousands of Cuban teachers. But that's inaccurate. What we brought was our experience and the program. It was Venezuelan volunteer teachers who organized and led the classes. More than 1.5 million Venezuelans have now been

49. Mission Robinson is named after Simón Rodríguez, who served as teacher to Simón Bolívar. Rodríguez's pseudonym was Robinson Crusoe, which he chose because of his enthusiasm for the novel by Daniel Defoe.

taught to read and write. It won't be that long before the country can declare itself a Territory Free of Illiteracy.

But the education program didn't stop there. It continued with Mission Robinson II. This program is what we in
Cuba called the Battle for the Sixth Grade. In Cuba it lasted
close to ten years. Ten years, to organize for everyone in the
country to reach the sixth grade. In Venezuela they're confident they will do it in closer to two years, using audiovi-
sual materials. The classrooms for Mission Robinson II are
already built.

Then there's Mission Ribas, which involves continuing on
and obtaining a high school diploma. And Mission Sucre,
which involves close to 400,000 high school graduates who
formerly had no access to the university.[50] These graduates
have been given scholarships to study and work, as well as a
$100 monthly stipend. And with that they're able to enroll at
the university. The government took a number of administrative buildings that had previously belonged to PDVSA and
created the Bolivarian University in Caracas.

That's the educational program.

As for medical assistance, after Barrio Adentro got started,
Chávez said that anyone who wants Cuban doctors in their
neighborhood should just say the word. Because the opposition was trying to block the Barrio Adentro program in states
and municipalities they controlled.

Within four or five months, Cuba sent 10,000 doctors to
Venezuela. These doctors are working in the poorest neighborhoods. Through the Family Doctor system, more than 17

50. These programs were named after José Félix Ribas (1775–1815) and
    Antonio José de Sucre (1795–1830). Both were leaders of the fight
    for Venezuelan independence and for the independence of Latin
    America as a whole.

million Venezuelans now have access to treatment.[51]

Venezuela is redesigning its medical system, beginning with primary care, then polyclinics, then hospitals. There are also private clinics and hospitals, of course, but the big majority of working people have little or no access to them. The public health system is being redesigned based around preventive medicine. With care provided by a doctor who is right there in the neighborhood. Each one serves 120 families.

Six hundred diagnostic centers have been created, including thirty-five high-technology ones, with rooms for intensive therapy, dentistry, ophthalmology, rehabilitation, and clinical laboratories with state-of-the-art equipment.

In addition to the doctors, there are several thousand Cuban dentists. Other services are being set up as well, such as eye care. One of the difficulties Mission Robinson ran into was that many people who had trouble learning to read and write couldn't see well. So 300,000 pairs of glasses were sent, including progressive lenses, as well as vision-testing equipment. Thousands of patients with various diseases have come to Cuba for medical care. And there is a special plan for cataract and other eye diseases, called Operation Miracle.

Thousands of sports instructors are part of the Barrio Adentro plan, too. They're organizing physical education and recreation programs in the communities. They've organized popular sports, children's sports, and gyms for the elderly.

As part of Cuba's collaboration, there's also the program I'm involved in, developing intensive vegetable cultivation,

51. By mid-2005 there were some 15,000 doctors, 3,000 dentists, 1,500 optometrists, and 1,500 nurses, technicians, and other Cuban medical personnel. There were also some 6,000 Venezuelan medical personnel participating in the Barrio Adentro program.

that is, small-scale urban agriculture. Not just in Caracas but throughout the country.

Urban agriculture program

KOPPEL: How did it begin?

SÍO WONG: In 2000 the general director of the United Nations Food and Agriculture Organization (FAO) based in Rome, Mr. Jacques Diouf, who is Senegalese, was here in Havana. He toured our center, and I explained to him our program for developing organoponic agriculture.

In February 2003 Mr. Diouf went to Venezuela. A food security program exists between the FAO and Venezuela.[52] The oil company's attempted coup against Chávez had just been defeated, but there was a food crisis, since the owners of the big food warehouses had joined in the economic sabotage.

Diouf told the Venezuelan government that the fastest way to produce food was urban agriculture. Cuba was the country with the most experience in that, he said. Diouf suggested that since Chávez is a friend of Fidel Castro, he should call Fidel and ask him to send General Sío Wong to help.

Within 48 hours I was on a plane to Venezuela, together with Adolfo Rodríguez Nodals, the director of INIFAT [National Institute of Basic Investigation in Tropical Agriculture] as well as the National Urban Agriculture Group. Also assigned to the mission were Dr. Miriam Carrión Ramírez and Engineer Miguel Salcines.

Through an FAO project they've begun to develop organoponic agriculture in Venezuela. The initial idea was for us to

52. The UN Food and Agriculture Organization has a Special Program for Food Security, which "aims to help those living in developing countries ... improve their food security through rapid increases in food production and productivity."

be there for ten or twelve days to orient the specialists and then return to Venezuela every two or three months to check how the work is going. It actually was the other way around: we spent two or three months there and then I came back to Cuba for fifteen or twenty days to work here.

We arrived February 20, 2003. On February 25 we met with President Chávez to present our experiences. On March 15 the president inaugurated the Fuerte Tiuna organoponic farm, and on March 28 the Bolívar 1 farm in downtown Caracas.

Bolívar 1 is right in the middle of the city, near the two towers and the Caracas Hilton. The Venezuelans provided a patch, sort of like a park, that was previously full of garbage. As we were designing it, we tried to fit in with the surroundings. "We can't cut down those palm trees," I said. Then it occurred to us that we should make it like the nearby Plaza Venezuela, which is circular in design. So we built a water tank in the middle, with a fountain over it, and the beds are circular. It's really quite artistic.

This is an arduous job, because we face the same difficulties and widespread lack of understanding about organoponic cultivation that we faced here in Cuba.

But urban agriculture will more and more serve as a source of employment, in addition to becoming a source of food in Venezuela. These programs are going to have a real social impact.

Defending Venezuela, defending Cuba

WATERS: The U.S.-backed opposition is carrying out quite a campaign against the assistance Cuba is giving.

Sío WONG: A big slander campaign has been waged by the opposition to the Chávez government, targeting Cuban doctors above all. Cuban doctors, they claim, aren't qualified physicians. They're taking jobs away from Venezuelan doctors. The opposition has tried, without success, to accuse the Chávez government of using these doctors to "Cubanize" Venezuelan society.[53] A similar campaign is being waged in the United States, of course.

The four commercial television stations in Caracas all belong to the opposition. The government has one TV station, with the oldest and most obsolete equipment. Practically all the newspapers and radio stations in Venezuela belong to the opposition, as well. But its propaganda crusade has failed.

The opposition has tried to attack the quality of the care Cuban doctors are providing. They even alleged that a child died due to poor treatment. But a substantial layer within the population itself is taking responsibility to win broad acceptance for the program. Because not only does Barrio Adentro offer 24-hour-a-day medical care, but 105 different medications are being distributed free of charge. Insulin for diabetics, for one.

According to a recent study, these volunteer doctors are seeing 1.5 million patients a month and have saved an estimated 7,000 lives. What's considered a life saved? It's when the person would have died had medical treatment not been applied in time. Either because the person didn't get to the doctor in time, or due to lack of money.

In 2003 CNN made a big ruckus about some Cuban doctors defecting. There were 10,000 Cuban doctors in Venezuela then. Three or four took off. What percentage is that? If U.S.

53. In June 2003 the Venezuelan Medical Federation (FMV) filed suit asking the courts to bar Cuban doctors from practicing. A lower court decision granting the request was overturned by higher courts. In July 2005 several hundred FMV members held a protest in downtown Caracas claiming Cuban volunteers are taking the jobs of Venezuelan doctors.

doors were suddenly flung open and every Venezuelan, Colombian, and Mexican who wanted a visa were granted one, how many do you think would go? Because many people in Latin America want to go to the U.S. in hopes of having a better life, from an economic point of view.

The medical and literacy programs, Barrio Adentro and Mission Robinson, have had a tremendous social impact.

I lived in Venezuela for almost a year, and I was able to observe the change. When we were building the first organoponic in the downtown park there, I asked some workers, "How come you're not with Chávez? If the previous governments haven't done anything for you in forty years, why aren't you supporting Chávez?"

The response back then was: "I don't support him because for three years Chávez hasn't given me a thing. I'm still poor."

But a transformation in popular opinion is under way. All these social and economic programs have created a shift. That's the reality.

When I arrived in Venezuela, I was one of the first Cubans who climbed the *cerros* of Caracas. Rather, I should say that I was one of the first *Fidel Castro* Cubans, since there are other kinds of Cubans there. I spent several days wandering through there to determine where to build an organoponic farm. As in many Latin American cities, the *cerros* are the poor areas, where no one else ever ventures. No one who doesn't live in the favelas in Rio de Janeiro ever enters those areas, for instance. Not even the police—or when they do, it's with guns blazing. The same with the Tepito neighborhood in Mexico City.

But in Venezuela we coordinate plans with the people from those communities, and they themselves organize security. The Cuban doctors are more protected and secure than almost anyone, because the residents themselves look after them.

I remember a recent program on Venezolana de Televisión—the state channel—where they were interviewing a resident of one of those communities. "Look, I'm not a Chavista," the man said, when he learned the crew was from Venezuelan Television. "But if anyone lays a finger on the Cuban doctor, he's going to have me to answer to. Because she saved my son's life." That's typical of the popular reaction.[54]

This is our modest contribution to the Bolivarian revolution. It shows the internationalist spirit we've been educated in. Earlier we said we were trained in that spirit because we're paying a debt to history. A debt to those Africans, to those Chinese, to those from the Dominican Republic, from Venezuela, from the United States, from Poland, all of whom fought in Cuba's wars of independence. So we have that duty. Our doctors and other volunteers go to Venezuela with the same spirit in which our internationalists went to Angola, Ethiopia, and Nicaragua.

The other day Chávez spoke about how he'd met with some Cuban doctors and then decided to send them some mattresses, some beds. Because he'd been informed that some of them were sleeping on the ground.

So a Cuban went up to him and said, "Mr. President, we want to live as they live." And he wouldn't accept the mattresses.

"That doctor taught me a lesson," Chávez said.

WATERS: The Cuban doctors and other volunteers are also

---

54. There have been a handful of incidents of physical attacks on Cuban internationalist doctors. A doctor was killed in Araguá state in 2003, and a Venezuelan assistant to a Cuban medical volunteer was killed in Caracas the next year.

learning many lessons about the realities of capitalist society.

SÍO WONG: Yes, they are. The three of us—Chui, Choy, and myself—lived under capitalism. We know what it is. But young people here born since 1959 don't know. Now they're living it. Now they're seeing people who lack money to pay for medicine, who lack money to pay for school, who lack money to pay for food. They see people without a job. That's the reality they see. And they ask themselves how this could happen in a country that produces three million barrels of oil a day.

The imperialists say we're subverting Latin America. They call us subversives. But the objective conditions in Latin America offer no way out. Argentina is an example. Bolivia is an example. Peru is an example. Ecuador is an example. Brazil. What can the imperialist system offer? What can capitalism, the neoliberal model or any other capitalist variant, give them? It has resoundingly failed throughout Latin America.

Millions live in the *cerros* of Caracas, and the people poured down from them to defend Chávez against the coup. The imperialists are afraid of those *cerros*.

When I was climbing those hills, people would come up and say, "We're all Chavistas here."

"I'm with Chávez too," I replied. "Fidel, Raúl, and Che made me climb a lot of hills. Now, in my late sixties, I'm still climbing hills. For Venezuela."

Perhaps they thought I was a Japanese journalist when they saw me with a camera.

No, I responded. "I'm a Cuban. I'm a Cuban of Fidel."

The Battle of Ideas

KOPPEL: You've referred to what is known in Cuba today as the Battle of Ideas. Can you explain what this is?

Sío WONG: Defenders of capitalism seek to impose their culture, their ideas, on everyone. They strip peoples all over the world of our own cultures. The imperialists possess supremacy in technology and science. Some they've developed, some they've stolen. They dominate the media and information systems worldwide, through which they attempt to impose their values and justify their social relations.

This is why the Battle of Ideas is so important and so complex. Our ability to wage this battle rests largely on education, on instruction, on culture. On the example we provide children and young people.

We're now beginning another revolution, this one in the education of our children. "One must be educated to be free," as Martí put it. How can our children, our young people, and consequently our men and women be truly free if they aren't educated to think for themselves? How can they contribute to the development of the country? The era of the manual, the blueprint is no more. We have to adjust things to our reality, and to the reality of the world today.

Before the revolution 95 percent of us here in Cuba, maybe more, considered ourselves anticommunists, even though we didn't know what socialism was. We were taught by comic books like Superman and Tarzan and Blackhawk. Blackhawk was one of our favorites. It was about a squadron of fighter pilots, and the characters included a Swede, a Frenchman, a . Chinaman, a Pole. They made the Communists out to be really bloodthirsty. The Chinese character, a cook named Chop-Chop, was a racist caricature. That's the type of thing they taught us, even at school. We lived that on a daily basis.

There's a famous story from the early years of the revolution about a meeting Fidel held with some peasants and workers.

"Do you agree with the urban reform?" Fidel asked them.

"Yes."

"Do you agree with the agrarian reform?"

"Yes."

"Do you agree with the nationalization of industry?"

"Yes."

"Do you agree with socialism?"

"Oh no, we don't agree with socialism!"

That's the way it used to be.

So what moment did Fidel choose to proclaim the socialist character of the revolution? He chose the opening of imperialism's attack on us at the Bay of Pigs in April 1961. It was then, as we buried our dead following the bombing of our airfields on April 15, that Fidel explained for the first time that our revolution is a socialist revolution. That air assault was the prelude to the mercenary invasion two days later.

As you know, most of the movies shown here in Cuba are made in the United States. We're not shut in. We don't live encased in a shell. People have access to the Internet, and they have relatives in the United States. There's been a broad development of tourism. The key thing is to teach ourselves to think.

Since the triumph of the revolution we've been educated in socialism. We've been educated in selflessness: to be capable even of giving our lives for another people. That's the highest expression of human selflessness.

I went to Angola to risk my life for the Angolan people's struggle. What material benefit was there in that? None. And that's how tens and tens of thousands went—teachers, doctors, specialists. They had to go through many difficulties, and in the most remote places. How is this possible without consciousness?

But by the late 1990s there were 76,000 young people in Cuba who weren't going to school or working. As Fidel said, we had been remiss. The majority of these young people had family problems with divorced mothers and fathers, and so on. We had started categorizing them as "predelinquents." This terminology was horrendous! How was it possible? They were born within the revolution. They are products of the revolution. They are our children. Their parents were the generation that had gone to Angola, to Nicaragua, and had given their lives for the revolution.

The truth is, there had been shortcomings in our educational work. There had been shortcomings in our political work. In our social work. We recognize this. I believe this is Fidel's genius—to recognize shortcomings and to take measures to correct them. And not lose a minute in the process.

With the opening of the Battle of Ideas, all these young people were encouraged to study, and they received a salary while doing so. The vast majority now believe they have a socially useful future.

This, I believe, is a cultural revolution. I don't like to use that phrase, since it brings to mind the Cultural Revolution in China. So let's call it an educational revolution. But that's what this great Battle of Ideas is: nothing other than a revolution within the revolution, so our entire people can get an integral and general education and culture.

I was explaining earlier that we have inequalities here that we don't like. More than 60 percent of the people here, for example, have access to hard currency. That means nearly 40 percent don't. I don't. But there are many people who do. They receive dollars or other convertible currency from their relatives abroad. Or they work someplace—such as in tourism, or in the tobacco, nickel, or electrical industries—that pays part of their wages in hard currency.

People often don't understand why prices are high at the dollar stores. I have to explain this to many people, including to businessmen who come here. These prices are set by the government to bring in hard currency, so we can pay for programs to compensate somewhat those who don't receive dollars. That's why prices in these stores are high.

We subsidize a number of items that everyone in Cuba has equal access to. Everyone receives medicines free of charge. Anyone here can have heart surgery without somebody asking about their bank account. Everyone receives education free of charge. Our social security not only provides retirement income for every single citizen but also covers disability, maternity, and pregnancy leave. Some friends criticize us for maintaining these programs. But we're demonstrating how much can be done with very limited economic resources. The key thing is the human resources.

This battle we're engaged in is undoubtedly complex, but it's vital. You have to see how our children, our young people express themselves, their political level. We want to spread that as widely as possible, to make culture and education mass activities, to defend our national identity, our socialist identity. Above all, we want to teach young people to think.

CHUI: One organization that has occupied a vanguard position in the Battle of Ideas is the Association of Combatants of the Cuban Revolution. This is an organization of those who have fought to advance the Cuban Revolution and its internationalist missions. Compañeros who were in the Rebel Army, the clandestine struggle, fought at Girón, in the struggle against the counterrevolutionary bandits, or carried out an internationalist mission, whether as a combatant or as a doctor or teacher.

All the combatants are assigned schools and workplaces, where we give talks and lead discussions with the students, workers, and the community. We discuss our experiences in the revolutionary struggle and on internationalist missions. We disseminate the history of the revolution and its contributions elsewhere.

But it's not primarily about the past. Our history is still being written. We continue fighting every single day for the unconditional defense of our socialist revolution.

That's why the Association of Combatants is in the front ranks of the struggle for the freedom of our Five Heroes, fighters against terrorism unjustly held prisoner in the jails of the United States. Just as we're on the front lines in denouncing the aggressive policies of the U.S. government toward our country.

CHOY: You've already heard our stories. You could write a book about Chui, about where he lived, where he worked. About how his father supported his family. The same with Moisés and how he was exploited by his brother-in-law. We know these things. We lived them. We suffered them.

Earlier I told you about the man who came into my father's store unable to feed his family because he didn't have seven cents. You heard about my friend who couldn't get into a dance because he was the son of a Chinese parent.

Nowadays young people don't see such things. They don't

live that kind of discrimination because of skin color, economic means, or anything else. We may not have the most adequate diet, but everyone in Cuba has breakfast, lunch, and dinner. All children and young people up to the ninth grade are guaranteed lunch at school. Before the revolution not everyone was assured even of being able to go to school. Much less get health care.

We have to educate the youth to know about these things. We have to educate them so they know about Cuba's history, about the independence war against Spain, the war against the Batista dictatorship, the glorious victory at Playa Girón, the struggle against the counterrevolutionary bands, the internationalist missions. So they really understand what a revolution is, what socialism is.

These young doctors, teachers, sports trainers, and others who go abroad on internationalist missions—they're getting an education about the type of social system these countries have. They're seeing that our system is very different. They are learning that yes, a better world is possible. But only with a socialist revolution.

CUITO CUANAVALE:
A VICTORY FOR
THE WHOLE OF AFRICA

We staked everything in Angola

FIDEL CASTRO

I BELIEVE THAT in the last twelve months, in the last year, our country has written one of the bravest and most extraordinary chapters of internationalism.

It all started less than thirteen months ago when the crisis developed in the People's Republic of Angola. It was a really difficult time; it was a particularly difficult situation for various reasons. We had been fulfilling our internationalist mission in that sister country for about twelve years. During those years in which we maintained our presence in Angola, we were true to our commitments not to participate in the internal strife, since each country must solve its own internal problems. Our presence was to serve as a shield against the South African threat, which is what gave rise to our presence in Angola in 1975, at the request of that country's leadership....

The crisis [late last year] stemmed from an offensive or-

This account by Fidel Castro of the battle of Cuito Cuanavale was presented to a rally of half a million people in Havana on December 5, 1988. The rally commemorated Armed Forces Day, December 2, the anniversary of the landing of the *Granma* in 1956, marking the beginning of the revolutionary war against the Batista dictatorship. The speech, excerpts of which are published here, appears in full in Fidel Castro, *In Defense of Socialism: Four Speeches on the 30th Anniversary of the Cuban Revolution* (Pathfinder, 1989).

ganized by the People's Armed Forces for the Liberation of Angola (FAPLA) against UNITA in southeast Angola, very far from the eastern end of our lines. Cubans were never involved in that offensive. This wasn't the first; there had been another offensive in 1985 from a point now known as Cuito Cuanavale.

Cuito Cuanavale was 200 kilometers east of the last point on the Cuban line, 200 kilometers from Menongue. It was where the 1985 FAPLA offensive against UNITA began toward the southeast. When they had advanced about 150 kilometers in that remote region, the intervention of South African forces came about, very far from our lines, 350 kilometers from the last point in our lines, forcing the FAPLA to fall back.

To tell the truth, we had our own views about those operations, and one of our viewpoints was that these types of offensives could not be undertaken without making allowances for South African intervention. We had very clear, very precise, and very categorical views on the issue.

There were no such offensives in 1986.

Our view was that if the aim was to undertake offensives along these lines inside Angola—which is an undeniable right of the Angolan government—the appropriate conditions had to be brought about to prevent South Africa from intervening. The appropriate conditions had to be brought about to prevent South African intervention! We told those advising such operations that they could not be carried out as long as the conditions were not brought about for preventing South African intervention.

Our views were heeded in 1986, but unfortunately they were not heeded sufficiently in 1987 and events unfolded just as we expected. At a given moment in those remote areas of eastern Angola, when the FAPLA offensive was successfully under way against UNITA, the South Africans again intervened with artillery, tanks, planes, and troops.

But in 1987 they did not limit themselves to intervening to stop the FAPLA. As had happened in 1985, this 1987 intervention occurred north of Mavinga. Mavinga is so far away that not even our fighter planes based in Menongue could reach it. As I was saying, this time the South Africans did not limit themselves to repelling the offensive. Instead they advanced toward Cuito Cuanavale in pursuit of the FAPLA and tried to destroy the largest and best group of Angolan troops. Cuito Cuanavale, as I said, is 200 kilometers east of Menongue, the eastern end of our lines. There the South Africans tried to decide the war against Angola in their and UNITA's favor.

Of course that faraway spot was not the ideal place for large battles since logistics and organizing supplies was very difficult. To get from Menongue to Cuito Cuanavale, you had to cover 200 kilometers through the jungle. In other words, the enemy had selected the field of battle that best suited it.

Once that situation had been created—a situation that in truth developed because our military views were not taken into account, a difficult situation that could prove to be decisive—then everybody asked us to act and try to avoid a disaster there. Everybody asked us to act and expected Cuba to solve the problem.

As we saw it, in point of fact, the Cuban forces and equipment in Angola were not sufficient to solve the problem. We didn't have enough men and equipment to defend a line more than 700 kilometers long, not to mention advancing 200 kilometers eastward through the jungle to deal with the problem. We ran the risk of becoming strong there and weak elsewhere, the risk of falling into a giant trap.

Therefore, from the start we saw the situation clearly. We concluded that although the problem could be solved, it was indispensable to reinforce the troops and apply an appropriate military conception. The principle was that you should not undertake decisive battles on terrain chosen by the enemy; you must wage decisive battles when you choose the terrain and strike the enemy in sensitive and genuinely strategic spots.

The crisis situation developed in mid-November. I had just returned from the Soviet Union, where I had attended the festivities surrounding the seventieth anniversary of the October Revolution. A few days after I got back, the news from Angola started coming in. The situation had become very critical, the South Africans were on the outskirts of Cuito Cuanavale, the threat was serious and there wasn't a minute to lose.

It was on November 15, 1987, when we met with the general staff of our Revolutionary Armed Forces and made the political and military decision to deal with the situation and take the necessary measures. To have done otherwise would probably have resulted in the annihilation of the best group of Angolan troops, with unforeseeable consequences for the survival of the People's Republic of Angola, as well as a complicated situation for our own forces. Therefore, after careful consideration, our party's leadership made the decision to reinforce the troops and help solve the serious problem.

But it wasn't so simple, it wasn't all so simple. There was a complex political situation. Comrade Gorbachev was to meet with President Reagan in Washington on December 7 to discuss important issues related to world peace. The action could be considered inappropriate. It was the worst possible time for a decision of this kind. The question was: either we make the decision or we face the consequences of letting the South Africans operate with impunity and decide the struggle in Angola militarily.

In all truth, the leadership of our party and the leadership of our Revolutionary Armed Forces never hesitated for even an instant. The correct decision was made on November 15, 1987, to be exact. The first thing we did was to send to Angola the most experienced pilots in our air force, to begin aerial actions from the base at Menongue against the South African forces besieging Cuito Cuanavale. Meanwhile, we selected and began sending from Cuba the combat units and necessary weaponry to meet the situation and foil the enemy plans.

The air force had a certain effect, but it wasn't enough. We had to fly in a group of advisers, officers, and cadres to Cuito Cuanavale, plus artillerymen, tank crews, and operators of arms and equipment. About 200 in all were sent in to provide support for the Angolans, chiefly technical and advisory support. But that wasn't enough, and by land we had to send tank, artillery, and armored infantry units 200 kilometers away. We had to safeguard Cuito Cuanavale and prevent the enemy from wiping out the Angolan forces and capturing the town, which was becoming a symbol of resistance and of the success or failure of South Africa.

That is how the battle unfolded—and I've mentioned only part of it. We weren't trying to make it a decisive battle. Next to Cuito Cuanavale, which is a municipal seat, flows the Cuito River. There was a bridge over it and the enemy, using sophisticated technology, employed drones and was finally able to make it impassable. So one part of the Angolan forces was on the other side of the river, without the bridge, and the other part was to the west, where the town of Cuito Cuanavale is located.

It was a complex situation, but not unsolvable. The enemy advance had to be stopped without giving them the chance to wage a decisive battle there. The enemy had to be stopped; they couldn't be allowed to destroy the group of Angolan troops and capture Cuito Cuanavale. A more detailed explanation will have to await another occasion and different circumstances. Perhaps it will be a task for writers and historians to give an explanation of exactly what happened there and how the events unfolded.

The Angolan government had assigned us the responsibility of defending Cuito Cuanavale, and all the necessary measures were taken not only to stop the South Africans but to turn Cuito Cuanavale into a trap, a trap the South African troops ran right into.

In Cuito Cuanavale the South Africans really broke their teeth and it all came about with a minimum of casualties—a minimum of casualties!—for our own forces, the Angolan and Cuban forces.

They were set on carrying out the action and they completely failed. But the Cuban-Angolan strategy wasn't simply to stop the enemy at Cuito Cuanavale, but to gather enough forces and equipment to the west of our lines to advance southward and threaten key positions of the South African forces.

The main idea was to stop them at Cuito Cuanavale and deal them blows from the southwest. Enough troops were gathered together to seriously threaten points of strategic importance for South Africa and strike hard at them on terrain that we, and not the enemy, had chosen.

Our troops advanced southward from the west, with enough men and equipment to fulfill their mission. It took only a few clashes with their scouting patrols and powerful air strikes at their positions in Calueque for the South Africans to realize the tremendous force they were up against, and this change in the relationship of forces was what paved the way for negotiations. No one should think that they came about by chance.

The United States had been meeting with Angola for some

time, presenting themselves as mediators between the Angolans and the South Africans to seek a peaceful solution, and so the years went by. But while these supposed negotiations were taking place with the United States as intermediary, the South Africans had intervened and tried to solve the Angolan situation militarily, and perhaps they would have achieved it if not for the effort our country made.

The fact is that the relationship of forces changed radically. The South Africans suffered a crushing defeat in Cuito Cuanavale and the worst part for them was still to come. The truth is that they started to play with fire and they got burned.

Perhaps never in these more than twelve years had they faced so much danger. When we reached the border of Namibia in 1976 we had men, we had a good number of tanks and cannons, but we had no air force or antiaircraft missiles and we lacked much of the equipment we have today.

I must say that our pilots covered themselves with glory in the battle of Cuito Cuanavale and wrote truly extraordinary pages in history. A handful of pilots went on hundreds upon hundreds of missions in only a few weeks. They had control of the air with the MIG-23s and we must say they carried out a great feat. That was an important factor.

We not only sent our best pilots to Angola, we also sent our best antiaircraft weapons, a large amount of portable antiaircraft equipment, a good quantity of antiaircraft missile artillery. We reinforced our air power and we sent as many tanks, armored troop carriers, and artillery pieces as were needed.

I mentioned the pilots, but it would also be fair to mention our tank crews' conduct, our artillerymen's conduct, that of our antiaircraft defense personnel, our infantry, our scouts, our sappers. They organized and helped set up impassable minefields where the South African tanks were blown up in

Cuito Cuanavale. Success was the result of the coordinated action of the different forces there, in close cooperation with the Angolan troops who really acted with extraordinary heroism and great efficiency in the common effort.

The Angolan 25th Infantry Brigade in particular distinguished itself in the battles waged east of the river. It was a common struggle with common merit and common glory.

In Cuito Cuanavale the greater part of the troops were Angolan; and in our southward advance, which we also undertook in common, the greater part of the troops were Cuban.

A truly powerful force was brought together. Air, antiaircraft, and land superiority was ours. We took great care to provide air cover for our troops and so, even when the South African planes vanished from the sky after receiving a few good lessons from our antiaircraft weapons, the troops always advanced and took up their positions with a maximum of antiaircraft support. And our antiaircraft weapons were and still are on maximum alert to prevent surprise attacks. We had thoroughly analyzed the experiences of recent wars and we did not give the enemy a single opportunity, not a single opportunity!

This was not just because of the measures we took on land—fortifying the field, the antiaircraft weapons, the planes—but we also performed construction feats. In a matter of weeks an airport was built for our fighters, an air base that enabled our planes to advance more than 200 kilometers and seriously threaten key spots of the South African troops. There was no improvisation, no adventures, no carelessness on our part. The enemy realized not just that they were up against very powerful forces but also highly experienced ones.

In this way the conditions were created that made possible the negotiations that have continued and have even progressed over the past few months. A radical change in the political, diplomatic, and military situation came about.

In these negotiations the United States has acted as mediator. You can say "mediator" in quotes, but this doesn't deprive its diplomatic action in these negotiations of a certain positive aspect. I say "mediator" in quotes because they are the allies of UNITA and provide weapons to UNITA; by doing that they act as the allies of South Africa. But at the same time, they're interested in seeking a solution to the Namibian problem, seeking some peace formula for the region that will lead to the withdrawal of Cuban troops from Angola.

We know that the United States had some sleepless nights over the kind of boldness whereby a small, blockaded, and threatened country like Cuba was capable of carrying out an internationalist mission of this nature. The empire can't conceive of this. They are the only ones in the world who are entitled to have troops everywhere, weapons everywhere, bases everywhere. And so the fact that a small Caribbean country was capable of providing support to a sister African nation is something beyond their parameters, concepts, and norms.

It's clear that this internationalist mission carried out by Cuba had a very big impact on Africa. The African peoples, and even African governments that are not revolutionary but belong rather to the right have viewed with admiration the mission carried out by Cuba in Africa. The African peoples know these are troops allied with them; they know that the only non-African country whose troops were sent to defend an African country against the aggression of racist and fascist South Africa is Cuba....

A large portion of our leadership's time, of my time, of the Revolutionary Armed Forces' time, was taken up with this problem throughout the year. I already told you it wasn't easy making that decision and, above all, I mentioned the moment when the decision was taken. I already told you in essence that it was on the eve of the Gorbachev-Reagan meeting. There were some who came to believe we were plotting against peace, plotting against détente, given the circumstances under which we felt compelled to send the reinforcements. But given the situation, I assure you we couldn't have lost a single day, we couldn't have lost a single minute. One minute lost and it would have been too late.

There are moments when difficult and bitter decisions have to be taken, and when that moment came our party and our armed forces did not hesitate for an instant. I believe this helped prevent a political calamity, a military calamity for Angola, for Africa, and for all progressive forces. I believe this decisively boosted the prospects for peace now present in the region.

I believe that on a day like today, tribute should be paid to the efforts made by our troops and by our people. This is a mission we can all feel proud of. It is one more page of glory for our fighting people, our armed forces, born on October 10, 1868, and reborn on December 2, 1956.

There are some who have even dared question the internationalist spirit and heroism of our people, who have criticized it. This is the Yankees' hope: that anti-internationalist currents would arise among our people to weaken us. As we have said before, being internationalists is paying our debt to humanity. Whoever is incapable of fighting for others will never be capable of fighting for himself. And the heroism shown by our forces, by our people in other lands, faraway lands, must also serve to let the imperialists know what awaits them if one day they force us to fight on this land here.

An unparalleled contribution to African freedom

NELSON MANDELA

THE CUBAN PEOPLE hold a special place in the hearts of the people of Africa. The Cuban internationalists have made a contribution to African independence, freedom, and justice, unparalleled for its principled and selfless character. From its earliest days the Cuban Revolution has itself been a source of inspiration to all freedom-loving people.

We admire the sacrifices of the Cuban people in maintaining their independence and sovereignty in the face of a vicious imperialist-orchestrated campaign to destroy the impressive gains made in the Cuban Revolution.

We too want to control our own destiny. We are determined that the people of South Africa will make their future and that they will continue to exercise their full democratic rights after liberation from apartheid. We do not want popular par-

This speech was given in July 1991, the year after Nelson Mandela's release from prison and barely two months after the last Cuban internationalist volunteers returned from Angola. Mandela paid a visit to Cuba to express thanks for Cuba's longtime support to the struggle of the South African people. His remarks, excerpted here, were presented to tens of thousands of Cubans and international guests at the July 26 celebration in Matanzas, Cuba, marking the 38th anniversary of the attack on the Moncada garrison. The speech is published in full in Nelson Mandela, Fidel Castro, *How Far We Slaves Have Come! South Africa and Cuba in Today's World* (Pathfinder, 1991).

ticipation to cease at the moment when apartheid goes. We want to have the moment of liberation open the way to ever-deepening democracy.

We admire the achievements of the Cuban Revolution in the sphere of social welfare. We note the transformation from a country of imposed backwardness to universal literacy. We acknowledge your advances in the fields of health, education, and science.

There are many things we learn from your experience. In particular we are moved by your affirmation of the historical connection to the continent and people of Africa. Your consistent commitment to the systematic eradication of racism is unparalleled.

But the most important lesson that you have for us is that no matter what the odds, no matter under what difficulties you have had to struggle, there can be no surrender! It is a case of freedom or death!

I know that your country is experiencing many difficulties now, but we have confidence that the resilient people of Cuba will overcome these as they have helped other countries overcome theirs.

We know that the revolutionary spirit of today was started long ago and that its spirit was kindled by many early fighters for Cuban freedom, and indeed for freedom of all suffering under imperialist domination.

We too are also inspired by the life and example of José Martí, who is not only a Cuban and Latin American hero but justly honored by all who struggle to be free.

We also honor the great Che Guevara, whose revolutionary exploits, including on our own continent, were too powerful for any prison censors to hide from us. The life of Che is an inspiration to all human beings who cherish freedom. We will always honor his memory.

We come here with great humility. We come here with great emotion. We come here with a sense of a great debt that is owed to the people of Cuba. What other country can point to a record of greater selflessness than Cuba has displayed in its relations with Africa?

How many countries of the world benefit from Cuban health workers or educationists? How many of these are in Africa?

Where is the country that has sought Cuban help and has had it refused?

How many countries under threat from imperialism or struggling for national liberation have been able to count on Cuban support?

It was in prison when I first heard of the massive assistance that the Cuban internationalist forces provided to the people of Angola, on such a scale that one hesitated to believe, when the Angolans came under combined attack of South African, CIA-financed FNLA,* mercenary, UNITA, and Zairean troops in 1975.

We in Africa are used to being victims of countries wanting to carve up our territory or subvert our sovereignty. It is unparalleled in African history to have another people rise to the defense of one of us.

We know also that this was a popular action in Cuba. We are aware that those who fought and died in Angola were only a small proportion of those who volunteered. For the Cuban people internationalism is not merely a word but something that we have seen practiced to the benefit of large

---

*A reference to the Angolan National Liberation Front led by Holden Roberto, formerly a pro-independence group, which was part of the imperialist-backed alliance seeking to topple the Angolan government.

sections of humankind.

We know that the Cuban forces were willing to withdraw shortly after repelling the 1975 invasion, but the continued aggression from Pretoria made this impossible.

Your presence and the reinforcement of your forces in the battle of Cuito Cuanavale was of truly historic significance. The crushing defeat of the racist army at Cuito Cuanavale was a victory for the whole of Africa!

The overwhelming defeat of the racist army at Cuito Cuanavale provided the possibility for Angola to enjoy peace and consolidate its own sovereignty!

The defeat of the racist army allowed the struggling people of Namibia to finally win their independence!

The decisive defeat of the apartheid aggressors broke the myth of the invincibility of the white oppressors!

The defeat of the apartheid army was an inspiration to the struggling people inside South Africa!

Without the defeat of Cuito Cuanavale our organizations would not have been unbanned!

The defeat of the racist army at Cuito Cuanavale has made it possible for me to be here today!

Cuito Cuanavale was a milestone in the history of the struggle for southern African liberation!

Cuito Cuanavale has been a turning point in the struggle to free the continent and our country from the scourge of apartheid!

The most profound tribute ever paid to our internationalist fighters

FIDEL CASTRO

IT WOULD NOT BE RIGHT for us to emphasize Cuba's modest contribution to the cause of the South African people, but on hearing Mandela's speech, compañeros, I believe that he paid the greatest and most profound tribute that has ever been paid to our internationalist fighters. I believe that his words will remain, as if they were written in gold letters, as an homage to our combatants. He was generous, very generous; he recalled the epic feat our people performed in Africa, where all the spirit of this revolution was manifested, all its heroism and steadfastness.

Fifteen years we spent in Angola! Hundreds upon hundreds of thousands of Cubans went there and thousands more went to other countries. That was the epoch in which imperialism would have given anything to see Cuba withdraw from Angola and end its solidarity with the peoples of Africa. But our firmness was greater than all the pressures and was greater than any benefit our country might have gained had we given in to imperialist demands—as if there

These are excerpts from Castro's speech in Matanzas, Cuba, July 26, 1991 immediately following the remarks by Nelson Mandela excerpted in the preceding pages. The speech is published in full in *How Far We Slaves Have Come!*

could ever be any benefit in abandoning principles and in betrayal.

We are proud of what we have done, and our troops came back from Angola victorious. But who has said this the way he has? Who has expressed it with such honesty, such eloquence? What we have not said, because basic modesty prevented us, he has expressed here with infinite generosity, recalling that our combatants made it possible for the sister republic of Angola to maintain its integrity and achieve peace; that our combatants contributed to the existence of an independent Namibia. He added that our combatants contributed to the struggle of the South African people and of the ANC. He said that the battle of Cuito Cuanavale changed the balance of forces and opened up new possibilities.

We were not unaware of the importance of the effort we made there from 1975 up to the last great feat, which was accepting the challenge of Cuito Cuanavale. This was at a distance greater than that between Havana and Moscow, which one can travel in a thirteen-hour nonstop flight. To get from Havana to Luanda is about a fourteen- or fifteen-hour flight, and Cuito Cuanavale was over in the southeastern corner of Angola, more than 1,000 kilometers from Luanda. That was where our country had to accept the challenge.

As Mandela was telling you, in this action the revolution staked everything, it staked its own existence, it risked a huge battle against one of the strongest powers located within the Third World, against one of the richest powers, with significant industrial and technological development, armed to the teeth, at such a great distance from our small country and with our own resources, our own arms. We even ran the risk of weakening our defenses, and we did so. We used our ships and ours alone, and we used our equipment to change the relationship of forces, which made success possible in that battle. I'm not aware of any other time when a war broke out at such a distance between so small a country and such a great power as that possessed by the South African racists.

We put all our chips on the table in that action, and it was not the only time. I believe we did the same in 1975, when we took an enormous gamble sending our troops to fight the South African invasion of Angola.

I repeat: we were there for fifteen years. Perhaps it should not have taken so long, because the way we saw it, that problem had to be solved; simply put, South Africa had to be prevented from invading Angola. That was our strategic conception: if we wanted peace in Angola, if we wanted security in Angola, we had to prevent South Africa from invading Angola. And if we wanted to prevent the South Africans from invading, we had to assemble the forces and the weapons necessary to prevent them from doing so. We did not have all the equipment to do this, but that was our conception.

The truly critical situation occurred in Cuito Cuanavale, where there were no Cubans at the time because the closest Cuban unit was about two hundred kilometers to the west. This brought us to the decision to employ the troops and the weapons necessary—on our own initiative and at our own risk—and to send whatever was necessary, even if it meant taking it from here.

Cuito Cuanavale is the site that became historic, but the operations extended along a line hundreds of kilometers long, and out of these operations a movement of great strategic importance toward southwest Angola developed. All of this is symbolized by the name Cuito Cuanavale, which is where the crisis began; but about 40,000 Cuban and Angolan soldiers with more than 500 tanks, hundreds of artillery pieces, and about 1,000 antiaircraft weapons—the great majority of these antiaircraft weapons of ours were transferred from here—advanced toward Namibia, supported by our air force and an airstrip constructed in a matter of weeks.

I'm not going to speak here about the strategic and tactical details of the battles; I'll leave that to the historians. But we were determined, together with the Angolans, to put an end to the invasions of Angola once and for all. The events turned out the way we had foreseen—and we don't want to offend or humiliate anybody—because when this new balance of forces developed (and by then we had assembled troops that were invincible and unstoppable), the conditions for negotiations were created, in which we participated for months.

We could have waged big battles there, but given the new situation it was better to resolve the problem of Angola's integrity and Namibia's independence at the negotiating table. We knew—how could we not know!—that those events would have a profound effect on the life of South Africa itself, and this was one of the reasons, one of the motives, one of the great incentives that pushed us on. Because we knew that once the problem in Angola was resolved, the forces that were fighting against apartheid would also benefit from our struggles.

Have we said it this way before? No, never, and perhaps we never would have said this, because, in the first place, we believe that above and beyond whatever international solidarity the ANC has had, above and beyond the enormous support from abroad—of public opinion in some cases, of armed action in our case—the decisive and determining factor behind the ANC's successes was the heroism, the spirit of sacrifice and struggle of the South African people led by the ANC.

This man, in these times of cowardice and so many things, has come to tell us what he told us this afternoon. It is something that can never be forgotten and it reveals the human, moral, and revolutionary dimension of Nelson Mandela.

Glossary of individuals, organizations, and events

Abreu, Gerardo (*Fontán*) (1931–1958) – A worker, he became a leader of Orthodox Youth. Head of July 26 Movement Youth Brigades in Havana from 1956. A leader of urban underground during revolutionary war. Captured, tortured, and murdered by dictatorship in February 1958.

Acevedo, Enrique (1942–) – Joined Rebel Army July 1957 at age 14. Later assigned to Che Guevara's Column 8. Served in Angola 1977 and 1987–88, commanding tank brigade. Brigadier general in Cuba's armed forces.

Agramonte, Ignacio (1841–1873) – Major general in Liberation Army, based in Camagüey province, during Cuba's first independence war against Spain. Killed in battle.

Aldana, Carlos (1942–) – Joined July 26 Movement at age 14. Served in Rebel Army. Member of Communist Party Central Committee 1980–92, serving on Political Bureau and Secretariat. Headed Cuba's negotiating team that settled terms with Pretoria and Washington in 1988 to end Angola war. Sanctioned and removed from all responsibilities 1992.

Almeida Bosque, Juan (1927–) – Bricklayer and Orthodox Party member in Havana at time of 1952 Batista coup. Recruited to movement led by Fidel Castro and participated in 1953 Moncada attack. Sentenced to ten years in prison. Released with other Moncada prisoners in May 1955 following successful national amnesty campaign. Participated in *Granma* expedition of November–December 1956. Promoted in February 1958 to commander. Headed Third Eastern Front. Since 1959 responsibilities have included head of air force, vice minister of Revolutionary Armed Forces, and vice president of Council of State. One of three Sierra combatants to hold rank of Commander of the Revolution. A member of Communist Party Central Committee and Political Bureau since its founding in 1965. Hero of the Republic of Cuba and president of Association of Combatants of the Cuban Revolution.

April 9 general strike attempt – On April 9, 1958, the July 26 Movement called a general strike across Cuba in attempt to topple the dictatorship. Announced without adequate preparation, the action failed. Batista's forces responded with stepped-up repression as well as a major offensive against Rebel Army positions in the Sierra Maestra.

Association of Combatants of the Cuban Revolution (ACRC) – Founded in 1993 as organization of combatants of Rebel Army, the urban clandestine struggle, Playa Girón, the struggle against counterrevolutionary bands, and Cuba's internationalist missions, both military and civilian. Composed of more than 300,000 members who work to transmit the history and lessons of the revolution to new generations.

Authentic Party (Cuban Revolutionary Party) – Bourgeois-nationalist party formed in 1934, popularly known as *auténticos*, claiming to be authentic followers of José Martí's Cuban Revolutionary Party. In power 1944–52 under presidents Ramón Grau and Carlos Prío. Key component of bourgeois opposition to Batista 1952–58. Organized armed wing known as Authentic Organization. After Batista regime fell, as revolution deepened during 1959–60, principal *auténtico* leaders left Cuba for U.S., where they joined counterrevolutionary forces.

Barredo, Lázaro (1948–) – Prominent Cuban journalist and writer. Has served as vice president of Union of Cuban Journalists and member of Executive Committee of Latin American Federation of Journalists. Currently vice president of International Relations Commission of Cuba's National Assembly.

Batista, Fulgencio (1901–1973) – A former army sergeant, he helped lead Sergeants' Revolt in September 1933, a military coup by junior officers in wake of popular uprising that had overturned dictatorship of Gerardo Machado weeks earlier. Promoted to colonel and chief of staff. Organized a second coup in January 1934, unleashing repression against workers, peasants, and revolutionary forces. After dominating several governments as army head, was elected president in 1940. Did not run for reelection in 1944, but retained base within army officer corps. Led coup on March 10, 1952, establishing brutal military dictatorship. Overthrown by advancing Rebel Army and popular uprising. Fled to Dominican Republic January 1, 1959.

Bolívar, Simón (1783–1830) – Known as the Liberator. Latin American patriot, born in Caracas. Led series of armed rebellions 1810–24 that helped win independence from Spain for much of Latin America.

Bordón, Víctor (1930–) – Member of Orthodox Youth and later July 26 Movement in Las Villas. Formed July 26 Movement guerrilla unit in Las Villas in late 1956 that in October 1958 was integrated into front led by Che Guevara. Attained rank of commander. Subsequently held national leadership responsibilities in Ministry of Construction in Matanzas. Director of Cometal Enterprise Group.

Bu, José – Chinese-born officer in Cuban independence army, serving at side of General Máximo Gómez. Fought in Cuba's 1868–98 wars of independence, reaching rank of lieutenant colonel.

Cabral, Amilcar (1924–1973) – Founder and central leader of African Party for the Independence of Guinea-Bissau and Cape Verde (PAIGC), 1956. In 1963 PAIGC took up arms against Portuguese rule, winning Guinea-Bissau's independence in 1974 and Cape Verde's in 1975. Assassinated January 1973.

Carreras, Jesús (d. 1961) – A leader of Second National Front of the Escambray. Joined armed counterrevolutionary bands in Escambray mountains after revolution's victory. Captured, tried, and executed.

Carrión Ramírez, Miriam (1945–) – Cuban agricultural scientist and researcher at INIFAT (Institute of Basic Research on Tropical Agriculture). Helped initiate small-scale agriculture project in Venezuela. Heads FAO Project there, and group of Cuban collaborators in it.

Castillo, Bárbara (1946–) – Cuba's minister of domestic trade. Member, Central Committee of Communist Party since 1991.

Castro, Fidel (1926–) – Student leader at University of Havana from 1945. A central organizer of Orthodox Party youth after party's founding in 1947. Orthodox Party candidate for House of Representatives in 1952 elections canceled by Batista following March 10 coup. Organized and led revolutionary movement against Batista dictatorship that carried out July 26, 1953, attack on Moncada garrison in Santiago de Cuba and Carlos Manuel de Céspedes garrison in Bayamo. Captured, tried, and sentenced to fifteen years in prison. His courtroom defense speech, *History Will Absolve Me*, was distributed in tens of thousands of copies across Cuba, becoming program of revolutionary movement. Released in 1955 after national amnesty campaign, he led founding of July 26 Revolutionary Movement. Organized *Granma* expedition from Mexico, late 1956, and commanded Rebel Army during revolutionary war. Following revolution's triumph, was Cuba's prime minister from February 1959 to 1976. Has been president of Council of State and Council of Ministers since then. Commander in chief of Revolutionary Armed Forces and, since its founding in 1965, the Communist Party of Cuba's first secretary.

Castro, Raúl (1931–) – An organizer of student protests at University of Havana against Batista dictatorship, he participated in 1953 Moncada attack. Captured and sentenced to thirteen years in prison. Released May 1955 following national amnesty campaign. A founding member of July 26 Movement and a participant in 1956 *Granma* expedition. Promoted to commander in Rebel Army, February 1958, and headed Second Eastern Front. Minister of the Revolutionary Armed Forces since October 1959. He is General of the Army, second-ranking officer of Revolutionary Armed Forces after Commander in Chief Fidel Castro. Vice premier from 1959 until 1976, when he became first vice president of Council of State and Council of Ministers. Since 1965 second secretary of Communist Party of Cuba.

Chávez, Hugo (1954–) – A lieutenant colonel in Venezuelan army, he headed failed military coup in 1992 and was imprisoned for two years. Organized new political party, the Fifth Republic Movement. Elected president of Venezuela, 1998; reelected 2000. Has used revenues from oil sales to finance numerous social programs that have won support of workers, peasants, and youth. Substantial numbers of these popular forces have repeatedly mobilized to block attempts by powerful sectors of Venezuelan bourgeoisie, with backing from U.S. government, to overthrow his government.

Chiang Kai-shek (1887–1975) – Leader of bourgeois Kuomintang (Nationalist) Party in China from 1925. Led massacre of workers that brought bloody end to second Chinese revolution 1925–27. From 1927 headed dictatorship, overthrown by 1949 Chinese Revolution. Subsequently dictator of U.S.-backed regime on Taiwan.

Chibás, Eduardo (1907–1951) – A leader of Student Directorate in fight against Machado dictatorship in 1920s and 1930s.
Member of Authentic Party. In 1947 founding leader of opposition Orthodox Party (Cuban People's Party), which had broad
popular support. Elected senator 1950. On August 5, 1951, in
act of protest against government corruption, shot himself at
close of radio address; died several days later.

Chomón, Faure (1929–) – Leader of Revolutionary Directorate
and survivor of March 13, 1957, attack on Presidential Palace.
Organized February 1958 expedition that established guerrilla front in Escambray mountains. Part of Las Villas front
commanded by Che Guevara after October 1958. Member of
Communist Party Central Committee since 1965; has served
as Cuba's ambassador to Soviet Union, Vietnam, and Ecuador.
A deputy in National Assembly of People's Power since 1976.

Cienfuegos, Camilo (1932–1959) – *Granma* expeditionary, 1956.
Captain in Rebel Army Column 4 led by Che Guevara, promoted to commander in 1958. From August to October 1958
led "Antonio Maceo" Column 2 westward from Sierra Maestra en route to Pinar del Río. Operated in northern Las Villas
until end of war. Became Rebel Army chief of staff, January
1959. Killed when plane lost at sea while returning to Havana,
October 28, 1959.

Cintra Frías, Leopoldo ("Polo", "Polito") (1941–) – From
peasant family near Yara, joined Rebel Army November 1957.
Finished war as a lieutenant. Volunteered for internationalist missions in Angola and Ethiopia in 1970s. Headed Cuba's
military mission in Angola 1983–86 and 1989. A Hero of the Republic of Cuba. Currently army corps general, head of Western
Army, and member of Communist Party Political Bureau.

Colomé, Abelardo (1939–) – Joined Rebel Army March 1957,
reaching rank of commander. In 1962–64 served as internationalist volunteer in Argentina and Bolivia to prepare for

and support guerrilla front in Argentina led by Jorge Ricardo Masetti. Headed Cuban mission in Angola 1975–76. Member of Communist Party Central Committee and Political Bureau, and a vice president of Cuba's Council of State. Interior minister since 1989. Holds rank of army corps general.

Cuban independence wars – From 1868 to 1898 Cubans waged three wars for independence from Spain. The Ten Years War of 1868–78, the "Little War" of 1879–80, and the war of 1895–98, leading to end of Spanish rule. U.S. government occupied Cuba in immediate aftermath of Spain's defeat.

Cuevas, Andrés (1915–1958) – Worker from village of Camajuaní in Las Villas. Joined Rebel Army early 1957, becoming captain. Killed at Battle of El Jigüe July 19, 1958. Posthumously promoted to commander.

Curita, El. *See* Sergio González

Díaz Argüelles, Raúl (1936–1975) – Member of Revolutionary Directorate from Havana, he joined Directorate guerrilla column in Escambray mountains 1958. Became Rebel Army commander. In early 1970s headed Revolutionary Armed Forces 10th Directorate, which oversaw assistance to Cuba's internationalist military missions. First head of Cuba's military mission in Angola in 1975. Killed by land mine December 1975 and posthumously promoted to brigadier general.

Dreke, Víctor (1937–) – Member of July 26 Movement in Sagua La Grande, Las Villas; joined Revolutionary Directorate column that coordinated actions with Che Guevara's Rebel Army column from October 1958 on. Commanded forces in Escambray mountains responsible for eliminating counter-revolutionary bands there 1960–65. In 1965 was second in command, under Guevara, of Cuban volunteer column in Congo. In 1966–68 led Cuban internationalists aiding national liberation forces in Guinea-Bissau. Later headed Political Directorate of FAR. Retired from active military duty with rank of colonel in 1990. Has held major responsibilities for Cuba's relations with Africa, including ambassador to Equatorial Guinea since 2003.

Espín, Vilma (1930–) – Founding member of July 26 Movement in Santiago de Cuba. Close collaborator of Frank País, helped organize November 30, 1956, uprising in Santiago and later served as July 26 Movement coordinator in Oriente province. Joined Rebel Army July 1958, serving in Second Eastern Front. President of Federation of Cuban Women since 1960. Member of Communist Party Central Committee since 1965 and Political Bureau 1980–91. Member of Council of State since 1976.

Espinosa, Ramón (1938–) – Member of July 26 Movement who joined Revolutionary Directorate guerrilla column in Escambray 1958, finishing war as first lieutenant. Served in Angola 1975–76, seriously wounded by antitank mine. Head of Cuban military mission in Ethiopia 1980–82. Since 1983 has been head of Eastern Army. Member of Communist Party Central Committee since 1980; Political Bureau since 1991. Holds rank of army corps general.

Fontán. *See* Gerardo Abreu

García, Guillermo (1928–) – Peasant from Sierra Maestra who became member of July 26 Movement cell. Helped organize regroupment of Rebel forces, December 1956. From early 1957, combatant in Column 1 led by Fidel Castro. Promoted to commander in Third Eastern Front led by Juan Almeida, late 1958. Member Communist Party Central Committee since 1965, Political Bureau 1965–86. Minister of transportation 1974–85. Member of Council of State. One of three Sierra combatants to hold title Commander of the Revolution.

Gómez, Máximo (1836–1905) – Born in Dominican Republic, he fought in pro-independence war in Cuba 1868–78. Major general of Liberation Army by end of conflict. When war relaunched in 1895, returned to Cuba as general in chief of Cuban independence army.

González, Sergio (*El Curita*) (1922–1958) – Trade union leader of Havana streetcar workers and bus drivers in late 1940s who joined Orthodox Party. In 1955 became founding member of July 26 Movement. During revolutionary war helped lead urban underground in Havana, managing printshop used by Movement. Former seminary student, was nicknamed "El Curita" (Little priest). Murdered March 1958 by Batista dictatorship.

Guevara, Ernesto Che (1928–1967) – Argentine-born leader of Cuban Revolution. Physician on *Granma* expedition. First combatant promoted to commander in revolutionary war. In 1958 led Rebel Army column from Oriente to Escambray mountains; united revolutionary groups in Las Villas province and led them in campaign culminating in capture of capital, Santa Clara. After 1959 triumph, in addition to ongoing military tasks, held responsibilities including head of National Bank and minister of industry; often represented revolutionary leadership internationally. From April 1965 led Cuban column fighting alongside anti-imperialist forces in Congo. In late 1966 led detachment of internationalist volunteers to Bolivia. Wounded and captured by Bolivian army in CIA-organized operation, October 8, 1967. Murdered the following day.

Herrera, Osvaldo (1933–1958) – Student leader in Santa Clara during fight against Batista, later active at University of Havana. Became Rebel Army captain, serving as adjutant to Commander Camilo Cienfuegos. Sent to Holguín June 1958 to reorganize leadership of July 26 Movement urban underground. Taken prisoner, he committed suicide rather than provide information.

Jordan, Thomas (1819–1895) – General in Confederate Army during U.S. Civil War. In 1869 as supporter of Cuban independence movement, led expedition of 300 men that landed in Cuba. Became general in Liberation Army and chief of staff. Later returned to United States.

July 26 Revolutionary Movement – Founded June 1955 by Fidel Castro and other participants in Moncada attack, along with youth from left wing of Orthodox Party and other forces, including Revolutionary National Action led by Frank País in Santiago and Revolutionary National Movement cadres Armando Hart and Faustino Pérez in Havana. During revolutionary war was composed of Rebel Army in mountains (*Sierra*) and underground network in cities and countryside (*Llano*—"plains"). In May 1958 national leadership was transferred from Havana and Santiago to Sierra Maestra, under direct command of Fidel Castro.

Kuomintang (Nationalist Party) – *See* Chiang Kai-shek

Lage, Carlos (1951–) – Vice president of Cuba's Council of State and secretary of Executive Committee of Council of Ministers since 1992. Member of Communist Party Central Committee since 1980, and member of Political Bureau. A physician, he headed Cuban Medical Contingent in Ethiopia in mid-1980s. Served on Fidel Castro's Coordination and Support Team.

Lazo, Esteban (1944–) – A farmworker from Matanzas, he joined Association of Rebel Youth following 1959 victory. Joined predecessor of Communist Party in 1963. First secretary of Communist Party in City of Havana province 1994–2003. Vice president of Council of State since 1992. A member of party's Central Committee and Political Bureau, he has been in charge of ideological matters for it since 2003.

Leyva, Enio (1936–) – Leader of July 26 Movement Youth Brigades in mid-1950s, responsible for organizing in high schools. In 1956 became head of action and sabotage in Havana. Went to Mexico in 1956 and was slated to be part of *Granma* expedition, but was arrested by police. Active in support of revolutionary struggle from Mexico. Returned to Cuba in 1959. Joined Revolutionary Armed Forces, becoming brigadier general.

López, Antonio "Ñico" (1934–1956) – Leader of Orthodox youth movement and then of pre-Moncada revolutionary movement led by Fidel Castro. Participated in July 26, 1953, attack on Bayamo garrison. Escaped arrest and lived in exile in Guatemala, where he met Ernesto Guevara in 1954 and helped win him to July 26 Movement. In 1955–56 was member of Movement's National Directorate and headed its Youth Brigades. Participated in *Granma* expedition in December 1956. Captured and murdered by army shortly after landing.

López Cuba, Néstor (1938–1999) – From peasant family near Holguín, he joined July 26 Movement in 1957 and Rebel Army in May 1958. Wounded while heading tank contingent at Playa Girón. Served on internationalist missions in Syria 1973, Angola 1975–76. After 1979 headed Cuba's military mission to Nicaragua during war against U.S.-backed counterrevolutionary forces. At his death a division general of FAR, member of Central Committee of Communist Party, and chief executive officer of Association of Combatants of the Cuban Revolution.

Maceo, Antonio (1845–1896) – Military leader and strategist in Cuba's 19th century wars of independence from Spain. Popularly known in Cuba as the Bronze Titan, led 1895–96 westward march from Oriente that culminated in Pinar del Río province. At conclusion of first war in 1878, became symbol of revolutionary intransigence by refusing to put down arms in an action that became known as the Baraguá Protest. Killed in battle.

Machado, Gerardo (1871–1939) – Led brutal U.S.-backed dictatorship in Cuba 1927–33. Elected Cuba's president in 1924. Forcibly extended term in office in 1927, unleashing protests across Cuba, which were brutally suppressed. August 1933 revolutionary upsurge brought down dictatorship and sent him into exile.

Mambí – Fighters in Cuba's three wars of independence from Spain between 1868 and 1898. Many were freed slaves and other bonded laborers. The term "mambí" originated in 1840s during independence fight from Spain in nearby Santo Domingo. After a Black officer in the Spanish army named Juan Ethninius Mamby joined freedom fighters there, colonial forces began calling guerrillas by derogatory name "mambíes." Later "mambises" was applied to Cuban fighters, who adopted it as badge of honor.

Mandela, Nelson (1918–) – Leader of anti-apartheid struggle and African National Congress of South Africa. Founder of ANC Youth League, 1944, and ANC's military wing, 1961. Arrested in 1962 and imprisoned until 1990. Released amid advancing revolutionary struggle, given major boost by apartheid army's defeat in Angola in 1988. Elected president of South Africa in country's first post-apartheid election in 1994, serving until 1999.

Marcano, Luis (1831–1870) – Born in Dominican Republic, he became general in Cuban independence army. Killed in battle.

March, Aleida (1934–) – Member of July 26 Movement urban underground in Las Villas. In late 1958 went to Escambray mountains. Joined Rebel Army Column 8. Widow of Che Guevara.

Márquez, Juan Manuel (1915–1956) – Imprisoned during 1930s for opposing Machado dictatorship. A founding leader in 1947 of Orthodox Party and its left wing. Joined July 26 Movement 1955. Second in command of *Granma* expedition. Captured days after landing and murdered.

Martí, José (1853–1895) – Cuba's national hero. A noted revolutionary, poet, writer, speaker, and journalist. Founded Cuban

Revolutionary Party in 1892 to fight Spanish colonial rule and oppose U.S. designs on Cuba. Organized and planned 1895 independence war. Killed in battle at Dos Ríos in Oriente province. His anti-imperialist program and broader writings are central part of Cuba's internationalist traditions and revolutionary political heritage.

Martínez Gil, Pascual (1943–) – Member of July 26 Movement during struggle against Batista. Headed Ministry of Interior Special Troops in Angola 1975. Member of Communist Party Central Committee 1980–89, deputy minister of interior 1980–89, and division general. Arrested 1989 on charges of abuse of authority and improper use of government funds and resources; sentenced to 12-year prison term.

Martínez Hierrezuelo, Miguel Mariano – Prominent combatant in July 26 Movement's clandestine struggle in Santiago de Cuba. Participated in November 30, 1956, uprising in support of *Granma* landing. Served as combatant in Rebel Army Column 1 under Fidel Castro; later in Third Front commanded by Juan Almeida.

Masetti, Jorge Ricardo (1929–1964) – Argentine journalist who traveled to Sierra Maestra in January 1958 and was won to Rebel cause. Founded Cuba's Prensa Latina news service after 1959. Died while leading guerrilla group in northern Argentina.

Mella, Julio Antonio (1903–1929) – Founding president of Federation of University Students (FEU) and leader of university reform movement in Cuba in 1923. A founding leader of Communist Party of Cuba in 1925. Arrested by Machado's police in 1926, he escaped to Mexico, continuing to organize against dictatorship. Joined international campaigns to defend Sacco and Vanzetti, Augusto César Sandino, and others. Hounded by Machado's agents, he was assassinated in Mexico City, January 1929.

Moncada attack – On July 26, 1953, some 160 revolutionaries under command of Fidel Castro launched insurrectionary attack on Moncada army garrison in Santiago de Cuba and simultaneous attack on garrison in Bayamo, opening revolutionary armed struggle against Batista dictatorship. After attack's failure, Batista's forces massacred more than fifty captured revolutionaries. Fidel Castro and twenty-seven others, including Raúl Castro and Juan Almeida, were tried and sentenced to up to fifteen years in prison. They were amnestied May 15, 1955, after a broad national campaign demanding their release.

Moracén, Rafael (1939–) – Joined Rebel Army 1958. Served on internationalist missions in Congo-Brazzaville 1965–67, Syria 1973, Angola 1975–82. Holds rank of brigadier general. Hero of the Republic of Cuba. Head of international relations for Association of Combatants of Cuban Revolution.

País, Frank (1934–1957) – Vice president of Federation of University Students in Oriente. Central leader of Revolutionary National Action and later of Revolutionary National Movement (MNR). In September 1955 his organization joined July 26 Movement and he became its central leader in Oriente province, its national action coordinator, and head of its urban militias. Murdered by dictatorship's forces July 30, 1957.

Pardo Guerra, Ramón (1939–) – Joined Rebel Army 1957; served in Column 8 under Che Guevara 1958. Member of Communist Party Central Committee 1965–86 and since 1997. Served internationalist mission in Angola 1980. Division general in Cuban armed forces. Head of national general staff of civil defense since 2002.

Paz, Ramón (1924–1958) – Member of July 26 Movement and Rebel Army commander in Column 1. Killed in battle of Providencia, July 28, 1958.

Pérez, Crescencio (1895–1986) – A member of July 26 Movement cell in Sierra Maestra prior to *Granma* landing. Among first peasants to join Rebel Army, finishing war as commander of Column 7. Following triumph of revolution, carried various responsibilities in Revolutionary Armed Forces.

Pérez Jiménez, Marcos (1914–2001) – Military dictator of Venezuela from 1952 until toppled in popular rebellion in January 1958.

Pino Machado, Quintín (1931–1986) – Member of July 26 Movement in Las Villas during revolutionary war. Responsibilities after 1959 included Cuba's ambassador to Nicaragua (1959–60), representative to Organization of American States, and vice minister of culture.

Plácido – Literary pseudonym of poet Gabriel de la Concepción Valdés (1809–1844). Arrested by Spanish colonial authorities, framed as ringleader of conspiracy to start slave uprising, and executed by firing squad.

Playa Girón – On April 17, 1961, 1,500 Cuban mercenaries organized, financed, and deployed by Washington invaded Cuba at Bay of Pigs on southern coast. In less than seventy-two hours of combat, mercenaries were defeated by Cuba's revolutionary militias, armed forces, and police. On April 19 remaining invaders were captured at Playa Girón (Girón Beach), the name Cubans use for the invasion and battle.

Popular Socialist Party (PSP) – Name taken in 1944 by Communist Party of Cuba. PSP opposed Batista dictatorship but rejected political course of Moncada assault and of July 26 Movement and Rebel Army in launching revolutionary war in 1956–57. PSP cadres collaborated with July 26 Movement in final months of struggle to topple dictatorship. After 1959 victory, July 26 Movement initiated fusion with PSP and Revolutionary Directorate in 1961, leading to founding of Communist Party of Cuba in 1965.

Portuguese revolution – In April 1974 Portugal's decaying military dictatorship, in power since 1926, was toppled in a coup by disaffected high-ranking officers. A key factor was the growing strength of liberation movements in Portugal's colonies in Africa, which was putting increasing strains on the regime and its military. The dictatorship's fall unleashed a revolutionary working-class upsurge that was diverted by Communist and Socialist parties into support for bourgeois forces, which consolidated new regime by early 1976. The 1974 coup became known as the Revolution of the Carnations, symbol of soldiers' refusal to fire on popular forces opposing the dictatorship.

Quesada, Gonzalo de (1868–1915) – Secretary of Cuban Revolutionary Party from founding in 1892. Representative in Washington of Cuban Republic in Arms during 1895–98 independence war. Later helped assemble and publish collected works of José Martí.

Ramos Latour, René (*Daniel*) (1932–1958) – July 26 Movement national action coordinator after Frank País's death, heading its urban militias. Joining Rebel Army as a commander in May 1958, he was killed in battle July 30, 1958, at end of Batista army's offensive in Sierra Maestra.

Reeve, Henry (*El Inglesito*) (1850–1876) – Union Army drummerboy during U.S. Civil War who went to Cuba and joined independence forces in 1869, inspired by Cubans' fight against slavery. Became a colonel and was named commander of Cienfuegos detachment of independence army. Killed in battle.

Republic in Arms – Created by Cuban independence forces in April 1869 at Guáimaro Assembly, to lead war against Spanish colonialism. First president was Carlos Manuel de Céspedes. In 1869 decreed abolition both of slavery and of indentured servitude.

Revolution of 1933 – A popular upsurge and revolutionary general strike toppled dictatorship of Gerardo Machado on

August 12, 1933. Through efforts by U.S. Ambassador Sumner Welles, Machado was replaced by proimperialist government led by Carlos Manuel de Céspedes, son of the initiator of Cuba's independence struggle in 1868. On September 4 the Céspedes government was toppled in a coup led by noncommissioned officers, students, and civilians, sometimes called the "Sergeants' Revolt." A coalition government was formed known as the Hundred Days Government, which included anti-imperialist leaders such as Antonio Guiteras. The new government decreed the eight-hour day and measures contrary to U.S. imperialist interests, including annulment of the U.S.-imposed Platt Amendment. On January 14, 1934, with support of the U.S. embassy, Fulgencio Batista, army chief of staff, led a coup. Over next several years he combined buying off some anti-imperialist leaders with murderous repression against those refusing to buckle.

Revolutionary Directorate, March 13 – Formed in 1955 by José Antonio Echeverría and other leaders of Federation of University Students. Its cadres organized attack on Presidential Palace and Radio Reloj on March 13, 1957, in which a number of central leaders, including Echeverría, were killed. Adding "March 13" to name, it organized a guerrilla column in Escambray mountains in Las Villas in February 1958 led by Faure Chomón. That column subsequently became part of front commanded by Che Guevara. Fused with July 26 Movement and PSP in 1961.

Rius Rivera, Juan (1848–1924) – Native of Puerto Rico who joined Cuba's independence war in 1870, distinguishing himself in combat. With resumption of war in 1895, sought to organize armed expedition to fight for Puerto Rico's independence. When plan failed to materialize, he led armed expedition to Cuba and joined independence army. Became a major general.

Rodríguez, René (1931–1990) – Member of revolutionary movement led by Fidel Castro in 1952–53. *Granma* expeditionary in 1956. Served in Column 8 under Che Guevara. After 1959 took on a number of responsibilities and headed Cuban Institute for Friendship with the Peoples (ICAP) for many years. Member of Communist Party Central Committee from 1980 until his death.

Rodríguez Nodals, Adolfo (1945–) – Cuban scientist and general director of INIFAT (Institute of Basic Research on Tropical Agriculture). Head of National Urban Agriculture Group in Cuba.

Roloff, Carlos (1842–1907) – Born in Poland, he went to U.S. to fight in Union Army during Civil War. Moving to Cuba in 1865, became a fighter in Cuban independence army in 1868. In 1890s was chairman of Cuban Revolutionary Party in Tampa, Florida. With war's reinitiation in 1895, returned to Cuba and became major general in Liberation Army.

Rosales del Toro, Ulises (1942–) – Joined Rebel Army 1957, serving under Juan Almeida. Carried out internationalist missions in Algeria and Venezuela 1963–68, and Angola in 1976. A member of Communist Party Central Committee since 1975 and of party's Political Bureau. Formerly FAR chief of staff and first substitute of minister of FAR, with rank of division general. Since October 1997, minister of sugar industry.

Salcines, Miguel (1950–) – Irrigation specialist for Ministry of Agriculture. As head of a UBPC, developed a number of urban agriculture projects in Cuba, and has collaborated in small-scale agriculture project in Venezuela.

Savimbi, Jonas (1934–2002) – In 1960 joined organization advocating independence of Angola from Portuguese rule. Founded National Union for the Total Independence of Angola (UNITA) in 1966 and led it until his death in an ambush. *See also* UNITA.

Schueg, Víctor (1936–1998) – Joined Rebel Army 1958, serving under Raúl Castro. Served on internationalist mission in Congo 1965. Served in Angola 1975–76, as chief of general staff of Cuban military mission. Head of Central Army 1987–88. Held rank of brigadier general in FAR. Alternate member of Communist Party Central Committee 1980–86, full member 1986–91.

Second National Front of the Escambray – Armed group in Las Villas led by Eloy Gutiérrez Menoyo. Formed November 1957 on initiative of Revolutionary Directorate but expelled by Directorate in mid-1958 for robbing and terrorizing peasants in Escambray. Refused to collaborate with Che Guevara's forces and other revolutionary units. Most of its leaders joined counterrevolution after 1959.

Sékou Touré, Ahmed (1922–1984) – Leader of independence struggle from France in what is today Republic of Guinea, whose capital is Conakry. Became president of country at independence in 1958, serving until his death.

Slavery in Cuba – First brought to Cuba in 1517 by Spanish crown, slaves were primary source of labor in the sugar industry, constituting over a third of the island's population by the 1840s. International treaties banning the slave trade from 1817 on, as sugar production in Cuba was expanding, led to a chronic labor shortage that Spain sought to alleviate by bringing in Chinese indentured laborers. Following opening of Cuba's wars for liberation from Spain in 1868, the Republic in Arms decreed abolition of slavery and other forms of indentured servitude, incorporating all those who wanted to fight into the independence army. In 1870 Spain decreed gradual elimination of slavery. In 1880 the crown declared all remaining slaves to be bonded laborers under the "patronato" system. On October 7, 1886, the remaining 25,000 patrocinados were declared emancipated.

SWAPO (South-West Africa People's Organisation) – National liberation movement formed 1960 to fight for Namibia's independence from South African colonial rule. Fought with Cuban-Angolan forces in southern Angola. Has headed Namibian government since independence in 1990.

Territorial Troop Militia – Nationwide volunteer militia organized 1980 to help defend Cuba from threat of imperialist attack. Composed of 1.5 million workers, farmers, students, and housewives, who train in their free time and help finance their military expenses.

Tito, Josip Broz (1892–1980) – Head of Yugoslav Communist Party from 1939. Led partisan movement against Nazi occupation during World War II 1941–45. Prime minister and later president of Yugoslavia (1945–80).

Tolón, José (Lai Wa) – Chinese-born officer in Cuban independence army, fighting in Cuba's three wars against Spanish colonial rule. Reached rank of captain.

Torres, Félix (1917–) – Commanded PSP guerrilla column in Yaguajay, northern Las Villas; collaborated with Camilo Cienfuegos's Rebel Army column in late 1958.

Trejo, Rafael (1910–1930) – Student body president of University of Havana Law School. Killed by police September 30, 1930, during demonstration against Machado dictatorship.

UNITA (National Union for the Total Independence of Angola) – Founded 1966 as movement to fight Portuguese colonial rule, led by Jonas Savimbi. In 1975, as Portuguese colonial rule was collapsing, allied itself with apartheid South Africa and U.S. imperialism in effort to overthrow government of newly independent country led by Popular Movement for the Liberation of Angola (MPLA). Over next 25 years UNITA waged a terrorist war against Angolan government, killing hundreds of thousands. Following a peace agreement, UNITA participated in 1992 elections but repudiated results, resuming civil war.

The month after Savimbi was killed in an ambush in February 2002, UNITA signed ceasefire with Angolan government.

Urgency Courts – Formed in June 1934 under first Batista regime, these courts were set up to try political offenders, and were used against Batista's opponents. They were abolished after triumph of revolution.

Valdés, Ramiro (1932–) – A truck driver and carpenter, he participated in 1953 Moncada attack. Was sentenced to ten years in prison. Released May 1955 following amnesty campaign. *Granma* expeditionary. Became second in command of Rebel Army Column 4 in Sierra Maestra, later becoming its commander, and second in command of Column 8 under Guevara in Las Villas. Minister of interior 1961–68, 1979–85. Member of Communist Party Central Committee since 1965, Political Bureau 1965–86. One of three Sierra combatants to hold title Commander of the Revolution.

Van Heerden, Neil (1939–) – Director general of apartheid South Africa's Ministry of Foreign Affairs in 1980s. Involved in negotiations with Cuba and Angola over end of Angola war. From 1996 to 2005 served as executive director of South African Foundation, representing 60 of country's largest capitalist firms.

Villegas, Harry (*Pombo*) (1940–) – Joined Rebel Army 1957, becoming member of Che Guevara's escort in Columns 4 and 8. Served with Guevara in Congo 1965 and later Bolivia, where he was a member of the general staff of the guerrilla movement. After Guevara was killed in October 1967, commanded surviving combatants who eluded encirclement by Bolivian army and returned to Cuba March 1968. Served three tours of duty in Angola in 1970s and 1980s. Brigadier general (retired) in Revolutionary Armed Forces, member of Central Committee of Communist Party, and deputy in National Assembly. Executive vice president of Association of Combatants of the

Cuban Revolution, heading its Secretariat of Patriotic-Military and Internationalist Work. In 1995 received title Hero of the Republic of Cuba.

Welles, Benjamin Sumner (1892–1962) – U.S. assistant secretary of state sent by President Roosevelt as ambassador to Cuba in 1933 to organize transfer of power from dictator Gerardo Machado and put an end to revolutionary upsurge. His efforts led to creation of proimperialist Céspedes government, which was toppled a few weeks later.

Wong, José (Huan Tao Pai) (c. 1898–1930) – Revolutionary from Canton, China, who arrived in Cuba around 1927 and became a leader of Workers and Peasants Protection Alliance, based in Chinese community. Joined Communist Party of Cuba and founded Chinese-language newspaper *Gunnun Hushen* (Worker-Peasant Call), serving as its editor. In May 1930 was arrested and imprisoned in Havana's Príncipe Castle together with other Communist Party leaders. Three months later, in an organized political assassination, he was strangled to death in jail cell by agents of Machado.

Youth Army of Labor (EJT) – Part of Cuba's Revolutionary Armed Forces, composed of detachments of youth who carry out agricultural, construction, and other work, at same time as they train militarily. Members receive pay corresponding to type of work they do.

Index

Abreu, Gerardo (*Fontán*), 21, 42, 43, 46, 47, 187
Acción Cívica Constitucional (Constitutional Civic Action), 28
Acevedo, Enrique, 94–95, 187
Africa: Cuito Cuanavale a milestone for, 83–84, 86, 99–100, 182; impact of Cuba on, 85, 89, 98–99, 151, 177, 179, 180, 181–82, 183; imperialist exploitation of, 100–101, 102, 181; slave trade, 3, 57, 58. *See also* Angola; Ethiopia; South Africa
African National Congress (ANC), 95, 184, 186
Agramonte, Ignacio, 61–62, 187
Agrarian reform, 123–24, 148
Agricultural Production Cooperatives (CPAs), 134
Agriculture: Cuban Revolution and, 123–24, 134; markets, 127, 138; organic, 132. *See also* Organopónicos; Urban agriculture
ALBA (Bolivarian Alternative for the Americas), 150
Aldana, Carlos, 96, 187
Algeria, 85
Almeida, Juan, 17, 37, 46, 54, 88, 187
Andropov, Yuri, 89
Angola: army of, 81, 86, 87, 169–70, 171, 172, 176; imperialist exploitation of, 100–101, 102–3; negotiations over, 83, 86, 94–96, 100, 174–75, 176–77, 186; South Africa and, 79, 80, 81, 83–84, 86, 87, 90, 92, 94–96, 170–71, 185; U.S. im-

perialism and, 79–80, 83, 92; war victims of, 81. *See also* Cuito Cuanavale
Angola, Cuban mission in, 5, 158, 163, 178; air force, 173, 175, 176, 179, 180, 186; command post in Cuba, 18, 88–89, 90; Cuban casualties, 83, 99; during 1975–76 stage, 79–81, 175, 181, 185; Fidel Castro's leadership of, 85, 88, 89–90, 93, 98, 177; historic place of, 80, 83–84, 86, 99–100, 177, 182, 184, 186; logistics of, 89, 93–94, 96–98; popular character in Cuba, 81, 98, 181; reinforcement of, 81–83, 86–88, 171–72, 173, 185–86; size and duration, 79, 85, 169, 183; Soviet Union and, 80, 81, 89, 93–94, 97, 170; strategic aims of, 79, 86, 92–93, 169, 185; strengthened Cuban Revolution, 100–101, 102, 104–5; and UNITA, 92–93, 170; voluntary character of, 85, 163. *See also* Choy, Armando; Chui, Gustavo; Sío Wong, Moisés
Apartheid. *See* South Africa
April 9 general strike attempt, 13, 29–30, 188
Argentina, 4, 75, 159
Association of Combatants of the Cuban Revolution, 6, 18, 88, 164–65, 188
Aúcar Jiménez, Antonio, 30
Authentic Organization, 50
Authentic Party, 188

CAPITALISM'S LONG HOT WINTER HAS BEGUN

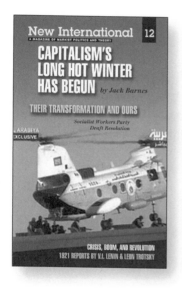

BY JACK BARNES

One of capitalism's infrequent, long winters has begun, explains Jack Barnes. We have entered the opening stages of what will be decades of economic and social crises and class battles. With the "acceleration of imperialism's drive toward war, it's going to be a long, hot winter. Even more important, slowly but surely and explosively, it will be one that breeds a scope and depth of resistance not previously seen by revolutionary-minded militants throughout today's world."

Also includes: "Their Transformation and Ours," Socialist Workers Party 2005 world political resolution, and "Crisis, Boom, and Revolution: 1921 Reports by V.I. Lenin and Leon Trotsky." $16

OUR POLITICS START WITH THE WORLD
BY JACK BARNES

The huge economic and cultural inequalities between imperialist and semicolonial countries, and among classes within almost every country, are produced, reproduced, and accentuated by the workings of capitalism. For vanguard workers to build parties able to lead a successful revolutionary struggle for power in our own countries, says Jack Barnes, our activity must be guided by a strategy to close this gap. "We are part of an international class that itself has no homeland. That's not a slogan. That's not a moral imperative. It is a recognition of the class reality of economic, social, and political life in the imperialist epoch."

Also includes: "Farming, Science, and the Working Classes" by Steve Clark and "Capitalism, Labor, and Nature," an exchange between Richard Levins and Steve Clark. $14

New International

A MAGAZINE OF MARXIST POLITICS AND THEORY

NEW INTERNATIONAL NO. 11
U.S. Imperialism
Has Lost the Cold War

Jack Barnes

Contrary to imperialist
expectations at the opening
of the 1990s in the wake of the
collapse of regimes claiming to be
communist, workers and farmers
across Eastern Europe and the
USSR have not been crushed. Nor
have capitalist social relations
been stabilized. The toilers
remain an intractable obstacle
to imperialism's advance, one the
exploiters will have to confront
in class battles and war. $15

NEW INTERNATIONAL NO. 10
Imperialism's March
toward Fascism and War

Jack Barnes

"There will be new Hitlers, new Mussolinis. That is
inevitable. What is not inevitable is that they will
triumph. The working-class vanguard will organize
our class to fight back against the devastating toll
we are made to pay for the capitalist crisis. The
future of humanity will be decided in the contest
between these contending class forces." $14

NEW INTERNATIONAL NO. 7

Opening Guns of World War III: Washington's Assault on Iraq

Jack Barnes

The murderous assault on Iraq in 1990–91 heralded increasingly sharp conflicts among imperialist powers, growing instability of international capitalism, and expanding wars and preparations for war. $12

NEW INTERNATIONAL NO. 8

Che Guevara, Cuba, and the Road to Socialism

Articles by Ernesto Che Guevara, Carlos Rafael Rodriguez, Carlos Tablada, Mary-Alice Waters, Steve Clark, Jack Barnes

Exchanges from the early 1960s and today on the political perspectives defended by Guevara as he helped lead working people to advance the transformation of economic and social relations in Cuba. $10

NEW INTERNATIONAL NO. 9

The Rise and Fall of the Nicaraguan Revolution

Based on ten years of socialist journalism from inside Nicaragua, this special issue recounts the achievements and worldwide impact of the 1979 Nicaraguan revolution. It traces the political retreat of the Sandinista National Liberation Front leadership that led to the downfall of the workers and farmers government in the closing years of the 1980s. Documents of the Socialist Workers Party. $16

NEW INTERNATIONAL NO. 4

The Fight for a Workers and Farmers Government in the United States

The shared exploitation of workers and working farmers by banking, industrial, and commercial capital lays the basis for their alliance in a revolutionary fight for a government of the producers. $12

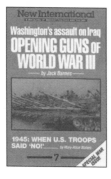

China and the Chinese Revolution

Marx and Engels on China and the Opium Wars

"Before many years pass away, we shall have to witness the death-struggle of the oldest empire in the world, and the opening day of a new era for all Asia."

Articles by Marx and Engels from the 1850s on European capitalism's plunder of China, the second Opium War waged by the colonial powers, and the place of the wealth and labor power wrested from China in the worldwide accumulation of capital. In *Collected Works of Karl Marx and Frederick Engels*, volumes 15 and 16. $35 each

By Any Means Necessary

Malcolm X

"There was a time when they used to say, 'He doesn't have a Chinaman's chance.' You don't hear that nowadays. When China became independent and strong, Chinese people all over the world became respected."

In eleven speeches and interviews, Malcolm X presents a revolutionary world perspective, taking up the proimperialist course of the Democratic and Republican parties, women's rights, U.S. intervention in Congo and Vietnam, the Cuban and Chinese revolutions, capitalism and socialism, and more. $16

Lenin's Struggle for a Revolutionary International

DOCUMENTS, 1907–1916;
THE PREPARATORY YEARS

Records the political battle led by V.I. Lenin in the decade before the 1917 Russian Revolution for a revolutionary course to oppose imperialist war by organizing to lead the toilers in overthrowing the capitalist rulers. Includes how proletarian revolutionists responded in the early 1900s to those in the world socialist movement who opposed opening the door to Chinese and Japanese immigration to America and Europe. $35.95

Leon Trotsky on China

Articles and letters on the Chinese revolution of 1925–27. Trotsky records the fight to reverse the disastrous course of the Stalin-led Communist International of subordinating the Communist Party there to an alliance with the capitalist-landlord Chinese Nationalist Party (Kuomintang). $34.95

CUBA AND AFRICA

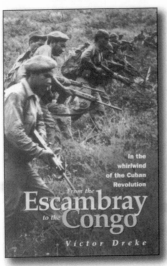

From the Escambray to the Congo
In the Whirlwind of the Cuban Revolution
VÍCTOR DREKE

The author describes how easy it became after the Cuban Revolution to take down a rope segregating blacks from whites in the town square, yet how enormous was the battle to transform social relations underlying all the "ropes" inherited from capitalism and Yankee domination. Dreke, second in command of the internationalist column in the Congo led by Che Guevara in 1965, recounts the creative joy with which working people have defended their revolutionary course—from Cuba's Escambray mountains to Africa and beyond. $17. Also in Spanish.

In Defense of Socialism

Four Speeches on the 30th Anniversary of the Cuban Revolution, 1988–89
FIDEL CASTRO

In talks to the people of Cuba and the world, Castro explains that economic and social progress is not only possible without the dog-eat-dog competition of capitalism, but socialism remains the only way forward for humanity. He presents a full account of the battle of Cuito Cuanavale, and the decisive place of Cuban volunteer combatants in the final stage of the struggle in Angola against the invasion forces of the South African apartheid regime. $15

Cuba's Internationalist Foreign Policy, 1975–80
FIDEL CASTRO

Castro discusses the opening year of Cuba's internationalist mission in Angola in 1975–76, as well as its military mission to Ethiopia. He also explains the historic importance of the revolutionary victories won by workers and farmers in Grenada and Nicaragua in 1979; relations with Cubans living in the U.S.; and the proletarian internationalism that guides the foreign policy of the Cuban government. $21.95

How Far We Slaves Have Come!
South Africa and Cuba in Today's World

NELSON MANDELA, FIDEL CASTRO

Speaking together in Cuba in 1991, Mandela and Castro discuss the place in the history of Africa of Cuba and Angola's victory in the battle of Cuito Cuanavale, and the resulting acceleration of the fight to bring down apartheid in South Africa. $10. Also in Spanish.

At the Side of Che Guevara
Interviews with Harry Villegas (Pombo)

HARRY VILLEGAS

Villegas worked and fought alongside Ernesto Che Guevara for a decade—in Cuba, the Congo, and Bolivia. A brigadier general in Cuba's Revolutionary Armed Forces, he talks about the struggles he has taken part in over four decades and explains the importance of Guevara's political legacy for a new generation around the world. $4. Also in Spanish.

The Diaries of the Revolutionary War in the Congo

ERNESTO CHE GUEVARA

Presents the lessons of the Cuban volunteer contingent that fought alongside anti-imperialist forces in the Congo in 1965 and discusses the prospects for revolutionary struggle in Africa. (Grove Press). $14.95.

CUBA

AND THE SOCIALIST REVOLUTION IN OUR EPOCH

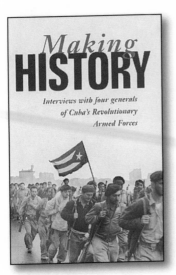

Making History

Interviews with four outstanding Cuban generals—Néstor López Cuba, Enrique Carreras, José Ramón Fernández, and Harry Villegas. A companion volume to *Our History Is Still Being Written*. Through these stories that capture half a century of revolutionary activity, we see the class dynamics that shaped the Cuban Revolution and the world. $15.95. Also in Spanish.

Episodes of the Cuban Revolutionary War, 1956–58

ERNESTO CHE GUEVARA

A firsthand account of the political events and military campaigns that culminated in the January 1959 popular insurrection that overthrew the U.S.-backed dictatorship in Cuba. With clarity and humor, Guevara describes his own political education. He explains how the struggle transformed the men and women of the Rebel Army and July 26 Movement, opening the door to the first socialist revolution in the Americas. $23.95

Aldabonazo

Inside the Cuban Revolutionary Underground, 1952–58

ARMANDO HART

In this account by a historic leader of the Cuban Revolution, we meet men and women who led the urban underground in the fight against the brutal U.S.-backed tyranny in the 1950s. Together with their comrades-in-arms in the Rebel Army, they not only overthrew the dictatorship. Their revolutionary actions and example worldwide changed the history of the 20th century—and the century to come. $25. Also in Spanish.

Playa Girón/Bay of Pigs
Washington's First Military Defeat in the Americas
FIDEL CASTRO, JOSÉ RAMÓN FERNÁNDEZ

In fewer than 72 hours of combat in April 1961, Cuba's revolutionary armed forces defeated a U.S.-organized invasion by 1,500 mercenaries. In the process, the Cuban people set an example for workers, farmers, and youth the world over that with political consciousness, class solidarity, courage, and revolutionary leadership, one can stand up to enormous might and seemingly insurmountable odds—*and win.* $20. Also in Spanish.

Cuba and the Coming American Revolution
JACK BARNES

"There will be a victorious revolution in the United States before there will be a victorious counterrevolution in Cuba." That 1961 statement by Fidel Castro remains as true today as when it was spoken. This is a book about the class struggle in the U.S., where the revolutionary capacities of workers and farmers are today as utterly discounted by the ruling powers as were those of the Cuban toilers. And just as wrongly. $13. Also in Spanish, French.

October 1962
The 'Missile' Crisis as Seen from Cuba
TOMÁS DIEZ ACOSTA

In October 1962, Washington pushed the world to the edge of nuclear war. Here, for the first time, the full story of that historic moment is told from the perspective of the Cuban people, whose determination to defend their sovereignty and their socialist revolution blocked U.S. plans for a military assault and saved humanity from the consequences of a nuclear holocaust. $24

Dynamics of the Cuban Revolution
A Marxist Appreciation
JOSEPH HANSEN

How did the Cuban Revolution occur? Why does it represent an "unbearable challenge" to U.S. imperialism? What political obstacles has it overcome? Written as the revolution advanced from its earliest days. $22.95

Also from
PATHFINDER

The Changing Face of U.S. Politics
Working-Class Politics and the Trade Unions
JACK BARNES

Building the kind of party working people need to prepare for coming class battles through which they will organize and strengthen the unions, as they revolutionize themselves and all society. A handbook for those repelled by the class inequalities, racism, women's oppression, cop violence, and wars inherent in capitalism, for those who are seeking the road toward effective action to overturn that exploitative system and join in reconstructing the world on new, socialist foundations. $23. Also in Spanish, French, Swedish.

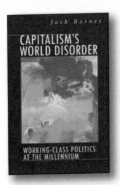

Capitalism's World Disorder
Working-Class Politics at the Millennium
JACK BARNES

The social devastation and financial panic, the coarsening of politics, the cop brutality and acts of imperialist aggression accelerating around us—all are the product not of something gone wrong with capitalism but of its lawful workings. Yet the future can be changed by the united struggle and selfless action of workers and farmers conscious of their power. $24. Also in Spanish, French.

The Communist Manifesto
KARL MARX AND FREDERICK ENGELS

Founding document of the modern working-class movement, published in 1848. Explains why communism is derived not from preconceived principles but from *facts* and from proletarian movements springing from the actual class struggle. $4. Also in Spanish.

Teamster Rebellion
FARRELL DOBBS
The 1934 strikes that built the industrial union movement in Minneapolis and helped pave the way for the CIO, recounted by a central leader of that battle. The first in a four-volume series on the class-struggle leadership of the strikes and organizing drives that transformed the Teamsters union in much of the Midwest into a fighting social movement and pointed the road toward independent labor political action. $19. Also in Spanish.

Thomas Sankara Speaks
The Burkina Faso Revolution, 1983–87
Colonialism and imperialist domination have left a legacy of hunger, illiteracy, and economic backwardness in Africa. In 1983 the peasants and workers of Burkina Faso established a popular revolutionary government and began to combat the causes of such devastation. Thomas Sankara, who led that struggle, explains the example set for all of Africa. $23

Problems of Women's Liberation
EVELYN REED
Six articles explore the social and economic roots of women's oppression from prehistoric society to modern capitalism and point the road forward to emancipation. $13

Lenin's Final Fight
Speeches and Writings, 1922–23
V.I. LENIN
In the early 1920s Lenin waged a political battle in the Communist Party leadership in the USSR to maintain the course that had enabled workers and peasants to overthrow the tsarist empire, carry out the first socialist revolution, and begin building a world communist movement. The issues posed in this fight—from the leadership's class composition, to the worker-peasant alliance and battle against national oppression—remain central to world politics today. $21. Also in Spanish.

Notebook of an Agitator
JAMES P. CANNON

Articles spanning four decades of working-class battles—defending IWW frame-up victims and Sacco and Vanzetti; 1934 Minneapolis Teamsters strikes; battles on the San Francisco waterfront; labor's fight against the McCarthyite witch-hunt; and much more. $26

America's Revolutionary Heritage
EDITED BY GEORGE NOVACK

A historical materialist analysis of the genocide against Native Americans, the American Revolution, the Civil War, the rise of industrial capitalism, and the first wave of the fight for women's rights. $22.95

The Struggle against Fascism in Germany
LEON TROTSKY

Writing in the heat of struggle against the rising Nazi movement, a central leader of the Russian revolution examines the class roots of fascism and advances a revolutionary strategy to combat and defeat it. $32

The Jewish Question
A Marxist Interpretation
ABRAM LEON

Traces the historical rationalizations of anti-Semitism to the fact that, in the centuries preceding the domination of industrial capitalism, Jews emerged as a "people-class" of merchants, moneylenders, and traders. Leon explains why the propertied rulers incite renewed Jew-hatred in the epoch of capitalism's decline. $20

John Coltrane and the Jazz Revolution of the 1960s
FRANK KOFSKY

John Coltrane's role in spearheading innovations in jazz that were an expression of the new cultural and political ferment that marked the rise of the mass struggle for Black rights. $23.95